People Strategies for Trainers

People Strategies
FOR
Trainers

176 Tips and Techniques for Dealing with Difficult Classroom Situations

Robert W. Lucas

AMACOM

AMERICAN MANAGEMENT ASSOCIATION

New York | Atlanta | Brussels | Chicago
Mexico City | San Francisco | Shanghai
Tokyo | Toronto | Washington, D. C.

Special discounts on bulk quantities of AMACOM books are available to corporations, professional associations, and other organizations. For details, contact Special Sales Department, AMACOM, a division of American Management Association, 1601 Broadway, New York, NY 10019. Tel.: 212-903-8316. Fax: 212-903-8083.
Web site: www.amacombooks.org

This publication is designed to provide accurate and authoritative information in regard to the subject matter covered. It is sold with the understanding that the publisher is not engaged in rendering legal, accounting, or other professional service. If legal advice or other expert assistance is required, the services of a competent professional person should be sought.

Library of Congress Cataloging-in-Publication Data

Lucas, Robert W.
    People strategies for trainers : 165 tips and techniques for dealing with difficult classroom situations / Robert W. Lucas.
        p. cm.
    ISBN 0-8144-7261-3
    1. Interpersonal communication.   2. Conflict management.
    3. Employees—Training of.   I. Title.
    HM1166.L83 2005
    658.3'124—dc22

                                                    2005002634

Printing number

10 9 8 7 6 5 4 3 2 1

To all of the wonderful, talented trainers, presenters, and educators who have provided guidance, advice, and support during my life and career.

Special thanks to my wife, friend, and life partner, MJ, for her love and encouragement. Also, to mother, Rosie, and my late father, Bill, who taught me the basics of life and encouraged me to always go further that I thought I could.

Thanks also to Jacquie Flynn and the members of the editorial staff at AMACOM for their experience and guidance in making this book a reality. Also, special thanks to Barbara Chernow and the staff of Chernow Services, Inc, for their expertise, professionalism, and dedication, which helped bring this project to a favorable conclusion.

Robert W. Lucas

Contents

SECTION IV Additional Issues

SECTION V Appendices

Introduction

This book is designed to be a user-friendly collection of practical and proven ideas and techniques for interacting with a variety of participant situations. The purpose of *People Strategies for Trainers: 176 Tips and Techniques for Dealing with Difficult Classroom Situations* is to identify the various types of difficult or uncommon classroom situations and learners that might be encountered and to provide some solid strategies for handling them. Because there is no perfect solution for dealing with problems in human behavior, the suggestions provided may work in some situations but not others. By choosing from all the techniques in the book, you should succeed in resolving most difficult classroom situations. A key point to remember is that because many of the strategies outlined can apply to various situations and learners, you should pick and choose whichever you believe to be most appropriate for a given situation. While some strategies are repeated for different categories of learners, I have not repeated every suggestion under each chapter in order to keep the text concise.

Over three decades of training adults and doing presentations, I have found that interpersonal communication skills and the ability to deal with a variety of people and personality styles are crucial in today's business environment. These skills are especially important to the success of anyone who is training or teaching others.

While many people have the opinion that no special skills are necessary to handle learners in a classroom, nothing could be further from the truth. As with any other skills, classroom management and the ability to effectively handle difficult people and situations require knowledge and training. If a participant situation is not handled in a timely and professional manner, it can easily disrupt learning for those involved, as well as for others who observe the situation. The challenge of effectively dealing with difficult situations is compounded by the fact that many people avoid conflict or confrontation when things get out of control or do not conform to the "plan." They simply do not or cannot deal with emotional issues. This is partly the result of their personality type and partly due to the fact that since childhood, many people are taught, "If you can't say something nice; don't say anything at all," "Be nice to others," or "It is better to run away and live to fight another day." Of course, the result is that people do not have the knowledge or feedback skills needed to deal with situations that fall outside the norm.

If you learn only one thing from this book, let it be that intimidation and coercion are short-term motivators and rarely resolve a situation. In fact, they often push the issue "underground." As a result, the problem festers and people harbor their emotions as they wait for a time when they can retaliate. Many adults often resent someone who tells them what to do. Most feel that they have earned the right to make their own decisions and control their own destinies. They are no longer children, who accept "because I said so" as a reason to do something. In fact, such an authoritarian, or parental, approach when dealing with adult learners is likely to cause resentment and escalate a negative situation. For that reason, I suggest that a non-threatening approach be used to deal with learners who create challenges in the classroom. Direct power, or control, should be used only when all other methods have been exhausted or when a real threat of imminent danger to you or others exists.

To assist you in dealing with a variety of people, learn about the various personality styles so that you can identify and appropriately respond to different types of behavior. Taking self-assessment behavioral style surveys can help you accomplish this goal; additional information is also available on the Internet. A second tool is to learn as much as possible about different cultures. Since we live in a global society, you are very likely to encounter people from different cultures. Each has a particular perspective on how a teacher and learner should interact, often based on cultural norms.

By establishing an environment in which distractions are minimized, learning is enhanced, and people have the opportunity to effectively interact, many classroom issues resolve themselves. In addition to specific hints on handling people found throughout this book, I have provided the following tools and suggestions for setting up an effective learning environment based on brain-based research:

- **Sample Training Agreement.** I use this actual agreement when conducting workshops. It can serve as a model for your own handout, poster, or slide to help set the tone for learning by outlining your roles and those of your participants at the beginning of a session.

- An overview of how **Dr. Abraham Maslow's Hierarchy of Needs Theory of Motivation** can be applied in training.

- Eleven **Classroom Seating Configurations** that can enhance learning, interaction, and communication, while facilitating more effective classroom management.

- **Creative Strategies for Effectively Forming Small Groups** that can add novelty, humor, and fun to a common classroom practice.

■ **Strategies for Creatively Selecting Volunteers** during training.

■ **Resources for Trainers, Educators, and Presenters** in the form of organizations that supply creative training and presentation products, books, and information.

■ **Web Site Resources** related to dealing with difficult participants, learners, and people in general.

For additional tips and strategies on creating an effective learning environment and adding creativity to training and educational environments, see my earlier book, *The Creative Training Idea Book: Inspired Tips and Techniques for Effective and Enhanced Learning.* You can also visit http://www.presentationresources.net.

Happy Training!

Robert W. Lucas

To contact the author:
blucas@presentationresources.net
blucas@globalperformancestrategies.com
1-800-308-0399 / 407-695-5535

SECTION I
An Overview

B efore starting any venture, it is a good idea to have a plan in mind. In this section, you will begin to explore some general issues related to working with learners in a variety of classroom situations. This includes discussions about why learners might behave in certain ways and tips on how to address their behavior.

CHAPTER 1

Defining the Challenge

If you ask a given group of trainers or educators to describe the most challenging or difficult type of learner or learner situation, you will get a variety of responses because what may be difficult to one person is not difficult to another. Even so, there are some common areas of behavior and participant characteristics that create difficulty in many learning environments.

A variety of factors affect the ability to deal with participant behavior. The following is a partial list:

■ Prior training related to handling difficult participant situations;

■ Experience of the trainer or educator;

■ Trainer/educator age and maturity;

■ Trainer/educator patience;

■ Personality type of the trainer/educator;

■ Trainer/educator cultural background (e.g., values and beliefs);

■ Trainer/educator desire/attitude toward dealing with difficult situations or people;

- Training or educational environment (e.g., room size and setup);

- Organizational culture (e.g., autocratic/bureaucratic versus laissez faire);

- Available time to deal with situations.

Challenging participant situations include learners with poor attitudes (e.g., those who do not want to be there or think they do not need the information being delivered), learners with overzealous attitudes (e.g., those who try to contribute too much or be too involved), learners for whom English is a second language, and learners with disabilities. Each type of learner presents different challenges and requires specific knowledge and skills to deal with effectively. Notice that I say "deal with," as opposed to "handle," which is often used to describe resolving such situations. My logic is that to be an effective trainer, facilitator, or educator, you must respect all learners and what they bring to the training or educational environment. Therefore, you learn to deal or interact with people, as opposed to "handle" (often associated with animals) them, which might come across as trying to control them. A learner's good and bad behaviors come as a package deal, as do a learner's personal characteristics. If you break through to your learners by winning their trust, while showing that you have their interests at heart, I believe that you can ultimately partner with most of them to succeed. Of course there will be those who do not and will not work with you for whatever reason(s). However, by demonstrating to your learners the **A**dded **V**alue **A**nd **R**esults **F**or **M**e (AVARFM) or by showing them what they will gain by cooperating with you and putting forth their best efforts, everyone benefits. A win-win situation is created, as you become successful at sharing information and skills with them and, as a result, they learn.

Some situations may require a more autocratic, disciplinary approach. If you encounter such an instance, try to at least salvage the relationship. You can potentially accomplish this by showing that while you may disapprove of the participant's behavior, you still respect the individual as a person. Another point is that if you fail to treat a difficult participant fairly, you may also lose their friends or colleagues in the room as they side with the learner.

WHY DIFFICULTIES EXIST

Adults are just kids with big bodies. They learn behaviors as children; they repeat the behaviors as adults. Unfortunately, many people had poor role models or did not learn positive behaviors when they were younger. In some cases, the role models did not mean to teach inappropriate behavior, they simply followed what they learned from their own role models, who also did a poor job teaching behaviors. Do you see a pattern here? Much of poor behavior can be traced to ignorance, complacency, or a lack of opportunity to gain effective knowledge or skills at some earlier point in their lives.

A second major issue for trainers is that the demographic makeup of any group of participants is likely to be varied because the population of the United States is increasingly diverse. For instance, for the first time in the history of the United States, the number of entry-level employees in the workforce from Latino cultures has surpassed that of other groups. Meanwhile, the number of people living in the United States who were born in other countries grows steadily. In effect, this means that many trainers, educators, and learners come from different cultural backgrounds. With this growth also comes the challenge of interacting with people who speak different languages and possess different values and beliefs than you do. For you and other trainers, the challenge is to design and deliver programs and materials that will be understood and successful. You also have to facilitate communication and understanding among the members of your groups.

Another challenge in training or educating people is that, as of 2004, more than 54 million people in the United States have some form of disability. As the general population ages, this number will surely increase. This fact requires that trainers and educators need to be aware of the special needs of many types of learners and be sensitive to their needs. It is important to recognize that difficulty in making accommodations for learners with disabilities often stems from ignorance on the part of a trainer or teacher as to what various disabilities are and any special needs they create. There is much research data and many advocacy groups from which you can educate yourself and learn strategies to make a learning environment a positive experience for everyone. One sample strategy for making the environment more positive and proactive is to be conscious of the way in which you and others refer to learners with disabilities. First, do not call attention to someone's disability. Treat all learners equally. Most people who have a disability do not want special treatment, they simply want an equal opportunity to learn and participate. If you must refer to a group or type of disability, always put the person before their disability. This places value on the person and relegates their disability to a simple fact, similar to someone having blue eyes, black hair, or other characteristic. You need to address the learning modalities of everyone through the use of appropriate and varied visual, auditory, and experiential learning materials and activities.

Here are some examples of forms of address. Others will be shown later in the book.

Instead of	Use
Blind people	Persons with sight impairments
The blind man/woman	The man or woman with a sight impairment
Epileptics	Person with epilepsy
Deaf and dumb person	Person with a hearing and learning impairment

Instead of	Use
Retarded person	Person with a learning impairment
Crippled person	Person with a mobility or dexterity impairment
Dyslexic person	Person with a learning impairment
Handicapped people	People with disabilities

COMMUNICATION AS A BASIS FOR PARTICIPANT BEHAVIOR

When I ask learners in trainer development programs to define situations that they consider difficult to handle, they often tell stories about inappropriate communication. This is not surprising when you listen to how adults teach children to communicate. Look at the following statements often used when talking to children to see if they sound familiar.

- Do it because I said so (in response to "Why can't I . . . ").
- Shut up and listen to me!
- Look at me when I'm talking to you!
- Children should be seen and not heard.
- Speak when spoken to.
- If I want your opinion, I'll ask for it.
- You must/have to . . . .
- That was a stupid thing to say.

When you think about such statements, which are often said in a harsh and autocratic voice, it is little wonder that classroom communication breaks down. How would you respond if someone used the language in these statements to you today? You would likely respond negatively or defensively. Many children do likewise. When such language is used on a regular basis throughout children's formative years, they might not know how to listen, ask questions, or give feedback effectively as adults. We try to hold learners accountable for communicating and interacting successfully in a training or educational environment, yet many do not have the tools required for such basic communication. Therefore, you must be patient and practice effective communication yourself in the classroom.

Communication is an important element of successful training and education. You can increase your effectiveness while reducing participant-related challenges by exhibiting positive interpersonal behavior. Here are some general strategies for dealing professionally with all types of participants.

 #1 Project a Positive Image

Like many things in your life, a positive attitude is crucial to success. The image that you project related to learners, your topic, session preparation, and the overall learning experience can often elicit similar participant behavior. For example, if you smile, appear approachable, and are open minded, your learners will likely reciprocate. On the other hand, if you exhibit apprehension, pessimism, or skepticism, you may dampen participant enthusiasm.

 #2 Words and Phrases
                    That Build Relationships

Here are some phrases that can assist in strengthening relationships within a learning environment. Such language reinforces your integrity and encourages learners to trust you more.

Please	You're right
Thank you	May I . . . ?
I can/will . . .	Have you considered . . . ?
How may I help?	I'm sorry
I'm sorry/ apologize for . . .	However, and, or yet (instead of *but*)
I was wrong	It's my/our fault
I understand/appreciate how you feel	Would you mind . . .
Situation, issue, concern *(instead of problem)*	What do you think?
Often, many times, some (instead of always or everyone)	

 #3 Treat Participants as Adults

Unlike children, adults usually have specific learning goals or agendas. As Malcolm Knowles and others have written, it is important to recognize the knowledge, skills, and experiences that your participants bring to your training sessions. Drawing on their talents and expertise enhances the learning environment for everyone. Ultimately, this results in respect and an appreciation for your learners.

 #4 Prepare for Brain-Based Learning

The 1990s have been referred to as the "Decade of the Brain" by many researchers, educators, and trainers because so many discoveries were made related to learning and brain functioning. Much of the research done since the early 1990s has focused on what factors stimulate the human brain, aid learning and recall, and ultimately can lead to application of what is learned.

According to findings, environmental factors, such as the use of toys, props, rewards, and active or experiential learning activities can enhance a participant's ability to learn material. Factors like room layout, type of furniture, color, lighting, use of music, plants in the room, smells, and temperature all impact the degree to which learning might occur. In general, you should build in ongoing activity and novelty to involve your learners and engage as many of their senses (sight, hearing, taste, smell, and touch) as possible throughout your sessions.

 #5 Listen Openly

As learners offer ideas, questions, suggestions, or feedback, take the time to patiently and objectively receive and think about their messages. Once you have done so, analyze what was said, then take appropriate action. Too often when learner feedback is perceived as challenging or argumentative, trainers and educators react defensively. If you really want learning to occur, to develop participant feedback and questioning skills, and to learn from them, establish a safe environment early in your sessions. Let learners know that their comments and opinions are welcome and that what happens in the room will stay there. This latter concept is often more crucial for internal trainers (those who are employed by an organization as opposed to ones hired to come in to provide training) who may have to overcome a perception that they represent upper management and will relay issues discussed in training to human resources or others in the organization. By establishing a safe environment and building trust and confidentiality, you can open a dialog with your learners.

#6 Provide Ongoing Feedback

In many training or educational situations, learners complain that their trainer, teacher, or facilitator did not give adequate feedback on their progress and that they did not receive proper instructions for activities. This is unfortunate because participants need to know how they are doing to gauge and improve their performances. They also need to know the rules and what is expected so that they can succeed and maximize their learning potential. The key to effective feedback is that it be appropriate, timely, and adequate.

ADDITIONAL FACTORS INFLUENCING PARTICIPANT BEHAVIOR

In addition to communication, many other factors impact classroom behavior. These often revolve around things like poorly learned time management skills, behavioral style preferences, culturally based behavior, personal abilities, physical and mental state, personal needs or wants, and experience. Again, many of these center on what participants have been taught or what they witnessed as "normal" behavior. Such behavior may have originated from caregivers, peers, or others in the environment in which the learners were reared. The following are ways in which the factors mentioned may impact the learning environment:

Impact of Poor Time Management Skills

Many people in urban societies, especially Americans, are very time conscious. For that reason, you often hear such phrases as "time is money," "faster than a New York minute," "time is of the essence," and "he who hesitates is lost." If some of your learners have poor time management skills, they can disrupt planned activities. They can also frustrate you and others in the room. The expectation of timeliness often drives people from a time-conscious culture to expect the same behavior of others. For example, in most business settings in the United States, anyone who is more than five minutes late for a meeting is often chastised. Because of cultural protocol, there are often rules or guidelines to which people are held accountable. For example, in many colleges and universities, etiquette often dictates that students wait no longer than 15 to 20 minutes when an instructor (depending on whether he/she is a full or associate professor) is late before leaving.

In some cases, the time management skills of your learners are a direct result of their environment or culture. Unfortunately, those from other cultures often value time differently. For example, it is not unusual for someone from an Arab country to be 30 or more minutes late for an appointment. A person from an Latino or Asian culture may be up to an hour late for an appointment. A phrase used by some people from India sums up the concept and justifies the lateness, "Indian standard time." Such tardiness is not viewed as disrespect for the time of others or rudeness; it is simply indicative of a cultural value or way of life.

In fact, in some Latin American countries, one is often expected to arrive late for an appointment or social function as a show of respect. To arrive at the scheduled time for a meeting or social event would be considered rude, because sponsors might be caught off guard and not be ready.

To compensate for differing perspectives of time, many trainers and educators plan accordingly and build in a bit of flexibility to their schedule. This is not to that you should not start and end of time. You should, since this sets the expectation of punctuality and keeps you on schedule. It is especially important to do so if your program or class is part of a larger conference or program agenda in which running over allotted time will cause a ripple effect that impact every trainer or educator that follows your session.

One way to build in flexibility and still stay on schedule is to plan activities that can be modified and still attain the desired outcomes.

For example, you can schedule a small group activity for a discussion but if you find that you are running short of time you can actually conduct an instructor-led activity which saves time of organizing and debriefing several small groups. A second technique for imbedding flexibility is not to cram every minute of your lesson plan with content. Instead, focus on several key issues and spend time reinforcing them through review and activities that help improve comprehension of how to apply what is learned. If something is "nice to know," but not crucial to program objectives, consider putting it at the end of the session or providing the information in a handout.

Impact of Behavioral Style

Attempts at categorizing behavior into types or temperaments have been going on for thousands of years. Like many facets of human behavior, a person's behavioral style can lead him or her to spend more or less time on an event or personal interaction. Some participants are more task focused, while others thrive on involvement with people in a training session. Such preferences can cause learners to be practical or obsessive in their behavior.

In addition, based on a personal style preference, some people are more friendly, outgoing, and willing to engage in self-disclosure. On the other hand, some styles lead to participants exhibiting quiet, withdrawn behavior that can negatively impact interaction. As a trainer or educator, learn as much about human behavior as you can in order to adapt your responses to learners and design programs that address the needs of all participants. Some common surveys used for determining behavioral style preferences are the Inscape Publishing Personal Profile System (PPS) and the Myers-Briggs Type Indicator.

Be sure to provide a variety of activities in your training or classroom so that both introverts and extraverts have an opportunity to express themselves and contribute to the learning environment. For example, open class discussions (large group) allow extroverts to claim center stage and share ideas or ask questions while small group activities and classroom groups give a forum for introverts to participate more comfortably. Since your goal should be to have everyone participate as much as possible and for all learners to get maximum benefit from the learning experience, plan your content delivery methods to include a variety of techniques.

Impact of Culture

Based on where participants have lived, they will display learned behavior based on the values (what is important) and beliefs (perceptions that one has about others, events, and situations) of their societies. For example, many people from Southeast Asia and Asia highly value training and education. As a result, teachers and trainers are often well-respected, valued, and almost revered. Other participants come from cultures where education and training are repressed (e.g., Iraq, Afghanistan, and other countries with repressive leadership). Still other learners may come from a country in which asking questions could cause the instructor to lose face (e.g., Japan and Korea). This might happen because of a perception that the instructor was not effective in communicating a point. The result is that such learners have little previous experience in open, free-communication learning environments and do not know the expected roles and expectations placed on learners.

Recognizing the cultural nuances of your participants and modifying your program and delivery style to meet their needs can enhance learning while reducing anxiety for you and your learners.

Some specific suggestions for addressing cultural differences include:

- At the beginning of your session or class, pass out a Training Contract (see Appendices) in which expectations are highlighted. Discuss these as a group at your first gathering.

■ Since many cultures value titles and formality (e.g. German and many Asian cultures), have learners identify how they would like to be addressed at the start of the first class or session. An easy way to accomplish this is to have them write their name they want to be called on a name tent or piece of paper that they tape to the front of their desk or table tent. If they choose Mr. or Ms. as a title along with their name, use this when addressing them. Do not assume familiarity or informality with them and start calling them by their first name (unless they tell you to do so), especially if they are older than you. This latter point is important because many cultures revere elders (e.g., North American Indians and many Latin and Asian cultures).

■ Provide activities in which learners can work in small groups since they are less likely to be self-conscious and may participate or offer ideas. This is especially true if they have difficulty with the English language. When grouping learners, always have them select a leader/spokesperson, or randomly do so yourself (see Appendices for suggestions) but allow people to "opt out" of the role if they prefer in order to prevent embarrassing them.

■ Be careful about asking specific questions of learners. Use broader group-focused questions to allow anyone to respond (e.g. who would like to give an example of? . . .

Impact of Personal Abilities

With the number of people with disabilities rising each year in the United States, you should prepare to accommodate the needs of learners who have special needs because of some form of disability. Based on the type and severity of disability, some participants may have difficulties in the learning environment with vision, hearing, mobility, dexterity, or processing information. Two examples of why it is important to consider these issues when training come from research. According to the Foundation of Children with Learning Disabilities, The United States has more than ten million children with learning disabilities. Other studies estimate that as much as five percent of the world's population is dyslexic (e.g., the brain is unable to effectively map alphabetic images and convert them to phonetic sounds). As these people and others with disabilities appear in your training and educational classes, they can pose challenges for themselves, you, and their peers.

Recognizing the need to accommodate learners with disabilities that are disclosed to you, and proactively doing so, is not only the correct thing to do, it is also the law in the United States (Americans with Disabilities Act of 1990 [ADA]).

Impact of Circadian Rhythm

Every person has a Circadian Rhythm. This is a naturally occurring 24-hour biological pattern by which people function. This internal "clock" often establishes the periods throughout the day when you are able to perform at your peak. Some people work best early in the day and are often called "morning people." They typically wake early, work feverishly through the morning into early afternoon , then start to slow down mentally and physically. By early evening, they are often ready for sleep. Others peak later in the day and are called "evening people." Unlike morning people, they struggle to get going in the morning but are ready to stay active late into the evening or early morning.

As a trainer or educator, recognizing that learners have different Circadian Rhythms is important in enabling you to plan activities and information in ways that allow best absorption by everyone. Failure to plan accordingly could mean that some learners miss out on key points because they are not mentally or physically alert. To accomplish this, you should keep your delivery style upbeat, and include novelty, fun, sound, and many of the other environmental and learning strategies addressed throughout this book. You goal should be to gain and maintain the attention of all your learners.

Impact of Physical and Mental State

In today's complex and hectic world, participants have much on their mind and are challenged to multitask throughout their week. In addition to workplace issues, they also wrestle with personal commitments and issues. All of this can lead to mental fatigue, distraction, and in some cases physical illness that decrease learning ability. As a trainer, you should be sensitive to verbal and nonverbal cues that might indicate that a participant is not ready to learn or receive information. If you suspect an outside or psychological distraction, discreetly discuss the issue with the learner during a break to see if you can do anything to enhance their learning potential. At some point, an option might be to suggest that the participant reschedule the training or class for a later time when they can focus attention on the program, if this is an option.

Other tactics for dealing with tired participants include making sure that your delivery style is high energy and that content is learner-centered. In other words, get participants actively involved through a variety of brain-based strategies. Become familiar with research on brain-based (active) learning and apply the concepts whenever possible to create an environment where learners are challenged mentally and kept alert.

Impact of Personal Needs and Wants

If you are familiar with Dr. Abraham Maslow's Hierarchy of Needs Theory as it applies to workers, then you are familiar with how people address their various levels of needs. In a learning environment, some people attend training out of necessity (they have to learn new skills to earn a living and keep their jobs or they were directed to attend), while others are looking to the future and want to increase their knowledge and skills to fulfill goals they have or take advantage of future opportunities. No matter why your learners come to training or class, your role is to identify and address their needs. You can determine some needs either by doing a needs assessment in advance (of learners, supervisors, peers, parents, customers, or whomever you can access) or once participants arrive in class (written or verbal questions and answers, icebreaker activities where they express why they are in training, or other creative methods for ascertaining information). You can also further recognize needs by talking to learners and observing them throughout training or class. There are specific tips related to applying Maslow's theory in the Appendices section.

Impact of Past Learning Experiences/Expectations

Lessons learned and experiences from the past can either enhance or detract from a learning experience. Because adults often base their expectations on events they have already experienced, they might come to training or class with preconceived ideas. For example, many adults who have not gone beyond high school and people from other countries may envision sitting in rows and having someone talk at them as a learning environment. Often, they have not experienced a learning environment in which they are asked for feedback, to express thoughts and ideas, or to take an active role in their own learning. That is why it is often helpful to set the stage for learning at the beginning of a program by explaining learning objectives, asking participants about their needs, and providing an environment that is upbeat and fun (e.g., props, festive decorations, color on the walls and tables, and a variety of training aids to stimulate learning). By expressing an expectation that they will participate and giving permission for them to experiment and have fun, you can set the stage for an enhanced learning experience for everyone (see Appendices for a Sample Training Contract that can help set expectations).

Preparing for
the Inevitable

It is not a matter of if, but when, you will encounter a participant situation that challenges your knowledge and skills as a communicator and facilitator. Such instances can either end in a successful transfer of knowledge or a frustrating learning experience for you and your learners. To reduce the likelihood that you will spend precious training or class time dealing with difficult situations, try the following preemptive strategies.

 #7 Prepare Yourself

To be an effective trainer or facilitator, you need many skills and a broad depth of knowledge. The more you know about training, development, and human learning, the more likely you are to assist in transferring knowledge from the learning environment to the real world (e.g., workplace or home) of your participants. Some of the areas in which you will need to become adept are:

■ Human behavioral styles, which are the behavioral tendencies that each person exhibits when interacting with others.
While much of a person's behavior is learned through experiences, education, values gained and other environmental
sources, some can be attributed to innate personality;

■ Human motivation, which refers to the internal drivers that
help individuals to focus their effort on attaining goals that
they set or meeting actual or perceived needs;

■ Concepts of adult learning that are derived from what
researchers such as Malcolm Knowles have learned about the
way that adults best gain and assimilate knowledge and skills;

■ Brain-based learning, which focuses on incorporating environmental and learning elements that scientists and
researchers have discovered stimulate the human brain.
Such strategies and techniques aid attention, memory, and
the brain best processes information;

■ Multiple intelligences, which is a term that Paul Gardiner
and other researchers have applied to the different levels
of learning that takes place within the human brain. Their
research indicates that learning is broken into many intelligences and that learners often have strengths in more than
one area. Gardiner has identifies eight different intelligences;

■ Training methodologies, which are the techniques used
by trainers to transfer knowledge and skills. These might
include such techniques might include such group activities
as discussions, role plays, and testing;

■ Active learning techniques that engage participants in a way
that they share responsibility for their own learning. Some of
the techniques might include games, movement, activities,
simulations, icebreakers, or other strategies that get people

actively involved and allow them to discover learning points on their own;

■ Creative thinking, which provides techniques or activities for people to "think outside the box" and explore various options. Many times, ideas are developed that are novel or even revolutionary;

■ Effective presentation/platform skills that include a sound understanding of how to prepare and deliver information to groups of people. Included in this category is the effective use of audio and visual training aids;

■ Interpersonal communication skills, which refer to basic tools for sharing ideas and gathering information. Examples are verbal and nonverbal communication, listening and questioning skills;

■ Training aid design and application, which refers to knowledge of various types of aids available and how to create or obtain and use them;

■ Training equipment usage that focuses on a basic understanding and familiarity with any training aids and equipment being used to support training or educational efforts;

■ Specific subject matter, which refers to an in-depth knowledge of whatever topic a trainer or educator is presenting so that they can answer learner questions.

 #8 Prepare the Environment

Much has been learned about the impact that the training environment has on the ability of participants to gain, retain, and recall information and use their skills. When possible, select training venues that:

■ Allow food, water, and other refreshments.

■ Have ample space to rearrange furniture and equipment and to maximize movement and visibility.

■ Permit the easy adjustment of lighting, electricity, and temperature to reduce distractions and aid efficiency.

■ Have windows that allow light without providing a portal for learners to look out and become distracted. Use blinds or arrange the room so that participants face away from windows so they get the benefit of the light without being distracted.

■ Have furniture arranged so that the entry doors are at the rear of the room and do not distract participants as people enter and exit. In additional, choose seating arrangements that provide maximum interaction between you and participants (see *Interactive Room Arrangements* in the Appendices section). By having access to and eye contact with learners, you can often control behavior through a variety of non-verbal cues which are discussed later in this book.

■ Give access for the set up of all equipment in advance and this ensures that everyone in the room can clearly see what is being presented.

 #9 Prepare Your Session
      Content and Delivery

The key to any successful learning event is to prepare in advance and consider possible contingency plans for a variety of situations. The following are a few ideas to help ensure that learning occurs:

■ Set realistic, attainable learning objectives for your sessions. Your learners should be able to see a direct correlation between the objectives and what they will learn in terms of their own situations. If they cannot, chances are that they will not buy into the program content and will become distracted in a number of ways. This can lead to distracting behavior.

■ Choose activities and learning strategies that add to, but do not distract from, learning. Plan ways to engage and keep learners interested throughout your sessions. One way to engage learners early in your session(s) is to plan an icebreaker activity in which they get to know one another, while disclosing things they like and/or do not like in a training session. You can then use their responses to avoid problems later. Here is a sample icebreaker:

—Have learners form groups of 4–5 people using one of the Creative Strategies for Grouping Learners in the Appendices section;

—Select group leaders using Creative Strategies for Selecting Volunteers in the Appendices section;

—Give each group 2 sheets of flip chart paper, masking tape and colored markers;

—Have each group member spend 10 minutes introducing himself or herself to peers in their group, then have the groups brainstorm two lists. On the first list, have them gather a list of things that they like to happen in a training session of class (e.g. positive feedback for ideas offered by learners). On the second list, have them identify things that they do not like to happen in a training or educational class (e.g. starting late);

—At the end of 10 minutes, have each group leader post their lists and in turn share what they have to the rest of the groups.

▪ Plan to develop and present guidelines or rules for the session. You can get better buy-in by having learners spend time at the beginning of a session developing their own list or adding to one you have already prepared. This list should contain such things as your roles and those of learners, break time protocol (e.g., returning on time), and guidelines for questioning and interaction. I sometimes present these guidelines in the form of a handout on colored paper with graphics called *Training Agreement* or *Training Contract* (see Sample Training Contract in Appendices).

▪ Develop attractive, professional handouts and training aids that complement your presentation and reinforce learning. Make sure to consider the possible needs of all learners (e.g., participants with English language deficits or those with various disabilities). Using such materials also helps ensure that participants with different learning modalities (e.g. auditory, visual and kinesthetic) and needs have access to information and can learn at their own pace and comfort level. By doing these things, you can potentially reduce the reluctance of some of your participants to become involved because they can better comprehend material and potentially increase their understanding of program content.

   Some easy ways to create useful handouts or training aids (e.g. slides) include using colored paper for single handouts or cover sheets for packets of materials since color attracts attention and stimulates the brain. On flip charts, this same impact can be attained through the use of various colored markers. Also, use graphics or clip art that relates to page content to visually reinforce written messages. This appeals to the visual learners in the group and adds a bit of fun and novelty.

▪ Consider creative strategies that you will use to group participants for activities and if necessary separate them in a seemingly random fashion (see *Creative Strategies for Grouping Learners* in the Appendices section).

- Plan creative strategies for selecting group leaders and volunteers so that you can involve participants in the learning (see *Creative Strategies for Selecting Volunteers* in the Appendices section).

- Practice, Practice, Practice! You cannot practice enough. Spend time rehearsing in the actual training environment that you will use for your session(s), if possible. Have the equipment and materials you plan to use in your training or class on hand so that you get used to manipulating and referring to them. Consider having other knowledgeable trainers watch your rehearsal and provide feedback.

FACILITATION HINT

To assist in gaining learner support and acceptance, consider spending time at the beginning of your session reviewing planned objectives. As you do so, ask learners how they see the objective(s) applying to what they do. You might also ask them what other objectives they have or what they want to gain from the session. Flip chart their ideas to make them visual and try to incorporate them into the training, if possible.

SECTION II
Environmental and Societal Issues

Many factors affect the ability of trainers, educators, and learners to effectively interact and influence the outcome of a learning activity or session. To negate or minimize these factors requires forethought, planning, and personal initiative on the part of the program facilitator. This section examines issues and elements that can influence learning and offers specific suggestions for effectively managing them.

Communicating with a Diverse Audience

The world community grows smaller each year as people from many cultures discover the need to come together and coexist. In the workplace, this means that you will likely encounter a variety of values, beliefs, needs, abilities, capabilities, learning and behavioral styles, and attitudes. To be successful in training such a wide array of participants, you will have to prepare to identify and meet their diverse needs. This means acquiring new knowledge and skills related to such things as the values, beliefs, cultural and subcultural preferences of people from various countries to apply in the classroom. Here are some general techniques to help increase your effectiveness when dealing with a widely diverse audience. Additional specific suggestions related to diverse individuals also appear in Chapter 4.

 #10 Respect Personal Preferences

Do not assume familiarity by addressing people by their first names until you have established an informal environment or relationship. To accomplish this, introduce yourself as people enter a session or explain at the beginning of the session that the program will follow a relaxed and informal format (if that is your intent), then request that each participant print the name by which others should address them. Whatever they write should be used until they tell you differently. For example, if someone writes Mr., Ms., or Dr. Wu, then address him or her as such. Unlike North Americans, who often tend to be more informal, people in many cultures covet and respect titles and academic credentials. Failure to recognize and honor this value could cause a learning and relationship breakdown.

 #11 Speak Clearly and Slowly

A participant who is trying to comprehend and translate your message into another language, or a participant with a learning disability, may struggle if words are spoken too quickly. According to research studies, the average adult in the United States speaks at a rate of approximately 125 to 150 words per minute. This equates to about as many words as an average written paragraph (as in this one) Anything faster may negate effective communication. Speak at a rate slow enough that allows your learners to understand without insulting them.

The easiest ways to determine if your message is being effectively understood is to watch your listener's nonverbal reaction (e.g. facial expressions) for signs of confusion. If you note such signals, pause, ask for questions or feedback, and repeat what you said in a different way, if necessary.

 #12 Use Open-Ended Questions

If your goal is to gauge understanding and increase communication, try questions that cannot be answered with a simple yes or no to encourage participants to voice opinions and increase dialog. This is important because the use of closed-ended questions (e.g. those that elicit short answers such as yes or no) get little information and may actually allow a participant to mask his or her inability to communicate in English. In fact, a closed-ended question like "Do you understand?" can be very offensive. Such a question could cause a learner to believe that you think he or she is not smart enough to comprehend your message. If you are unsure about whether a question is open- or closed-ended, remember that open-ended ones typically start with "what,""when," "why," "how," or "where" while closed-ended questions often start with an action verb, such as, "did," "would," "could," "should," "will," or "may."

 #13 Speak at a Normal Volume and Tone

Many times, trainers and educators unconsciously raise their voices in an effort to increase learner comprehension. This is not an effective tool for communication and will likely offend the participant(s). Just because someone speaks another language does not make him or her hearing impaired. Yelling or changing tone does nothing to enhance understanding and is potentially offensive.

 #14 Use Verbal Pauses

Short breaks or pauses in the flow of your message can improve comprehension. Using this technique can allow someone who speaks English as a second language or someone with a hearing, mental processing, or speech deficit to comprehend and respond to your messages. To help make this possible, pause frequently as you speak, particularly at the end of a sentence or thought. Pauses also allow your learners to translate what you have said into his or her own language, comprehend, then respond in English or ask questions.

 #15 Listen Patiently

You may have heard that patience is a virtue. It is also an important tool for ensuring that effective interpersonal communication is occurring between you and your learner(s). Take the time to focus on what a participant is saying and try to understand their intended message without interrupting them. If you are unsure of the person's intent, ask him or her for clarification in a non-threatening manner. Perhaps even ask if anyone else has a thought about what was said. Maybe someone else understood and can help you understand without embarrassing the participant. While you may feel frustration in such situations; imagine how the participant feels as others look on. Try to put everyone at ease while working toward better information exchange.

 #16 Use Nonverbal Cues Cautiously

As a trainer or educator in a global world, you would be wise to learn as much as you can about other cultures and the way people within them communicate and interact. Once you have done so, it is important to incorporate the findings into your training or classroom. Although many common nonverbal cues or signals are used throughout the world, their meaning is not always interpreted in the same way in each country, culture, or subculture. A symbol in one country may take on an entirely different meaning to someone from another area of the world. As examples of how different cultures interpret nonverbal gestures, the following are some common nonverbal hand gestures used in the United States that have different meanings in other countries.

GESTURE

"V" formed by extended index and middle finger (palm facing someone else). Note that in England and several other countries the gesture with palm away from someone is an obscene gesture.

UNITED STATES: Peace

BRITAIN, FRANCE, CANADA AND MANY OTHER COUNTRIES: Victory

BELGIUM: "I swear it"

GESTURE
Circle "O" formed with thumb and index finger with the remaining fingers extended,

UNITED STATES: Okay, all right, or acceptable

JAPAN: Money (coins)

BELGIUM AND FRANCE: "A big zero," lacking value, or worthless

GESTURE
Index finger extended upward by itself

UNITED STATES AND OTHER WESTERN COUNTRIES: The number 1, wait one minute. Also a way of beckoning someone or getting attention (e.g., trying to signal a restaurant server that you need him or her)

GESTURE
Hand made into a fist with the thumb pointing up

UNITED STATES: Used for hitchhiking (meaning going my way), okay, all right or "good going"

AUSTRALIA, BRAZIL, NEW ZEALAND, NIGERIA, AND SCOT-LAND: Vulgar gesture

JAPAN: The number five, reference to a male companion.

 #17 Always Introduce Activities in a Clear, Concise Manner

Take care to divide assignments or tasks into individual steps. Provide written, as well as, clear verbal guidelines using short sentences and words, with transitions from one point to the next. Doing this will increase your chances of success when communicating with learners who speak English as a second language. It also helps those learners who have disabilities which impact the receipt or comprehension of information and individual's who need more time to process data received.

　　Be clear and concise when providing directions and instructions. For example, do not simply gesture to a group of participants and say, "If you are on this side of the room, please pick up your materials and move to that side of the room." Instead, say, "If you are on my left, please pick up your materials and move to the near corner on the right side of the room for an activity." If you use language similar to the first example, people who are not paying attention or those with visual impairments may have no idea what you want done. As a result, they may take extra time in accomplishing the task, thus disrupting your schedule and creating the need for you to repeat directions. Another possibility is that they may simply be too embarrassed to ask and try to figure it out on their own, thus increasing their own frustration and their opportunity for failure.

 #18 Repeat Information When Necessary

If you are asked to repeat something, take your time and do so without appearing irritated or distracted. Remember that people who speak English as a second language and those with certain types of disabilities may not get every word spoken. They may also not fully comprehend the first time they hear something. This is why giving written information or instructions can also help during a session. Also, to increase the comfort level for learners who desire to ask questions, you may want to mention at the beginning of the session that they should ask for clarification if you are unclear. This does two things. First, it let's them know that it is okay to ask questions and secondly, it puts the responsibility for misunderstanding on you as opposed to their inability to comprehend or inattentiveness since you stress that you might be unclear in your communication.

 #19 Use Inclusive Language

When speaking to a group or addressing participants, be aware of audience demographics. Avoid terminology that could potentially exclude, isolate, or discriminate. For example, instead of using language like, "As you fellows, guys, or gals have found out . . . ," try referring to participants generically as, "Many of you have found out. . . . " This is a more inclusive approach and not likely to offend. People often adopt pet or favorite phrases or terminology outside of class that they use with learners in class (e.g. calling others "people," "you guys" or "folks"). This could be perceived as inappropriate, disrespectful or misunderstood by some learners. One way to determine if you use such language is to periodically audiotape or videotape your presentations and analyze them. Doing so helps you to identify and correct problematic language and can improve your delivery style overall.

 #20 Avoid Offensive or Discriminatory Jokes or Remarks

Related to inclusive language is the need to keep in mind that humor often does not easily transcend cultural boundaries or generations. Each participant has personal preferences and defines social accept-ability in ways based on their own value systems and learned prefer-ences. That does not make them wrong, just potentially different from you. Do not forget that while you may not agree with the views of others, you should respect all learners and their beliefs to main-tain credibility. This can also prevent you from alienating anyone in the room. In some instances, participants may have hidden sensi-tivities of which you are unaware. Jokes or comments that center on race, gender, nationality, culture, politics, religion, age, sexual orien-tation, height, weight, or other personal characteristics should therefore be avoided. This means that neither you nor anyone else in the room should communicate in such a way. As the session leader, learners look to you to ensure a safe environment where offensive language and behavior is not encouraged.

 #21 Watch Terminology

Just as titles, jokes, and remarks can offend, so too can some words or terms. It is a good idea to avoid words that focus on or single out a person or that might demean an individual or group. For example, instead of, "The black participant in the corner," you could say, "The participant in the corner with the blue shirt on" Or simply use the person's name since you had them identify themselves earlier in their introductions. Other terms that some people might find offensive include handicapped or crippled, boy, girl, idiot, ladies and gentlemen, and ma'am. These may conjure up negative stereotypes or project condescension to some participants.

 #22 Use Standard English

Technical terms, contractions (e.g., didn't, can't, wouldn't), slang (e.g., like, you know, dissed, bottleneck), or broken English (e.g., words or phrases that fail to follow standard rules of grammar or syntax) can be obstacles to someone who does not speak English well or those unfamiliar with the words or phrases (e.g. someone from another generational group that did not use the terminology).

It is sometimes helpful to recognize that some participants might understand English without being comfortable with colloquial expressions or being able to speak it fluently.

 #23 Encourage Participation by Everyone

In additional, they may prefer not to speak English (especially in large group settings) because they are either self-conscious about their ability or simply choose not to do so. One factor that could contribute to such behavior is that, unlike many Western cultures, learners from certain cultures value and use silence as an important aspect of communication. Instead the value of being humble and not taking a center position is a sign of respect and good manners. Many Westerners might interpret this to mean that the person does not understand what he or she has been told. Another possibility for lack of involvement may be personality style, mood, medical condition (e.g. illness like the flu), feelings about a topic, or lack of knowledge on the topic.

In order to enhance the learning opportunities for all participants try several of the strategies in this chapter to get learner involvement. Also, give everyone the opportunity to participate through small group activities or have learners anonymously write down their ideas, questions, suggestions, or concerns on strips of paper and pass them in to you. Select these randomly and read them aloud then, either respond to them or hold open discussions about them. For example, in a session on customer service, I sometimes have suggestions for making a customer feel welcome written down on small paper strips. These are collected and placed in a box or in something like a small ceramic word jar titled "Warm Fuzzies" (see http://www.presentationresources.net). This type of approach allows everyone to have input into session content and learning while allowing those uncomfortable with speaking up in class a chance to participate equally without a fear of embarrassment or peer criticism.

 #24 Avoid the Word "NO"

Unlike many North Americans, learners from some cultures (e.g., parts of Asia) are often careful not to offend, cause someone embarrassment, or to loose esteem or face in the eyes of others. For that reason, some languages do not even have a word for *no (for example Burmese)*. In instances where a negative response is required, a participant from some countries might say "Yes," or something like, "That may be difficult or impossible," instead of simply saying no.

This type of response prevents the other party from losing face (esteem) (e.g. Vietnam, Cambodia, India, or Korea). Being sensitive to this cultural variation can help prevent frustration within your learning environment.

#25 Use Care When Giving Constructive Feedback

Feedback on a performance should always be in a positive, assertive, and friendly manner. This is especially important when dealing with participants from other cultures because of the face issue mentioned earlier. If you must make corrections or give constructive feedback, try language that is not directed at the person, but at the behavior they are exhibiting. You may even want to take responsibility for the error. For example, if someone fails to correctly perform a task of fill out a form, you might say, "Maybe I wasn't clear about what I wanted you to do." Then, repeat your instructions.

#26 Allow Adequate Time for Movement and Task Completion

Each of your participants processes information at different speeds. Some people with mental or physical disabilities may not be able to think or react as quickly as others. For those reasons, consider building time into your programs for activity and task accomplishment. To do this, focus only on a specific number of key objectives or points rather than cramming too much content into the agenda. It is better to focus on quality and learning than to perform an information dump and hope people get it. Build in time for interim and final reviews of key concepts throughout your session or class. This increases the likelihood that all learners with "get it."

#27 Ensure That Written Materials Are Clear

You can accomplish message clarity by choosing a 12-point font (lettering) for your handouts. This is large enough to reduce eyestrain. If you know that you have a participant with a visual impairment, make a separate handout with a larger font or enlarge the original handout. Visual aids (e.g., slides, transparencies, and flip chart lettering) should be large enough to be seen anywhere in the room. Take the time to check this before learners arrive. There are advocacy group websites for people with sight impairments on the Internet that can offer technical guidance in this area.

Another consideration is the lighting in your classroom or training area. Lights that are too dim, too bright or improperly positioned and cast a shadow can make reading difficult for not only people with vision impairments but for anyone and can ultimately impact learning.

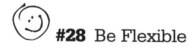

#28 Be Flexible

Even if you do not understand a learner's culture or language, use positive listening, as well as nonverbal and verbal techniques to enhance communication.

Part of your flexibility will come from recognizing that your views are not the way of the world. Making the mistake of believing that everyone has the same experiences and sees things as you do can lead to communication and relationship breakdown. Probably it is wiser to assume that participants from other cultures do not have the same knowledge base and experience. Therefore, share information with each other openly and freely. Listen for points of agreement or commonality.

CHAPTER 4

Participants Who Speak English as a Second Language

According to U.S. Census Bureau figures, there are estimated to be more than 26-million foreign-born people in the United States (9.7 percent of the population). As cultural boundaries melt in the workplace, your opportunities for interaction with participants for whom English is not the primary language increases. Additionally, as many jobs are exported to other countries and as multinational companies acquire more international holdings and partners, trainers and managers will be called on more often to be adept at dealing with employees from outside the United States. Educators will also have to contend with students who relocate to their area. Such situations can become frustrating if you are not prepared to deal with them.

 #29 Let Your Learner Guide the Conversation

Where interacting with someone who speaks English as a second language, let learners take the lead when they have questions, comments, or ideas. Give them an opportunity and adequate time to voice their thoughts without interrupting them. Some participants may take a while to get to know you and others in the room before feeling comfortable enough to ask a question or voice an opinion. This could be out of embarrassment about their language skills or fear of making a mistake or they may simply choose to remain silent. In fact, many cultures (e.g. Japanese) value and use silence as an important aspect of communication. This is something that many people from Western cultures find difficult to understand and disconcerting. Many times, when someone from the United States or other Western country encounters silence, they will immediately say something else to fill the uncomfortable void that they perceive. In fact the other person may simply be reflecting or translating their thoughts before responding. A typical, yet potentially inappropriate, Western perception to silence is the belief that the person who does not join in to a dialog does not understand what he or she heard. This may cause a relationship and communication breakdown as well as confusion on the part of both parties, especially if a comment is repeated or questions like "Do you understand? are inappropriately asked. To avoid this, it is best to wait for a period (e.g. 10–15 seconds) before repeating or asking a question.

Depending on where they were reared, some of these participants may take a rigid or formal approach and get right down to business by taking the lead. Still others may choose to have someone else act as a mediator or intermediary. In any event, recognize the cues and follow along when you can.

 #30 Listen Patiently

Recognize that while you may be frustrated, so is the learner. Take the time to focus on what he or she is saying and try to understand the intent of their message.

It is important not to appear impatient when learners are asking questions or making statements. You can potentially avoid the appearance of being impatient by consciously thinking about your nonverbal cues or behavior. For example, do not look at your notes or watch as the person speaks or interrupt to summarize what you believe to be their point. Let them finish what they are saying and then respond appropriately. Many times, someone speaking will pause only to have their facilitator or teacher try to provide a word for which they seem to be searching or to finish their thought in order to move along with planned activities. This is not only rude but can also diminish the possibility of involvement by all learners.

 #31 Speak Clearly and Slowly

Keep in mind that most adults in the United States speak at a rate of about 125 to 150 words per minute. While this may seem acceptable to you, it is fast for someone who is trying to get a message from you or someone else, translate it into their language, and then respond in English. This entire decoding and encoding process of messages takes time and it can feel frustrating if your learner feels rushed for an answer or does not have time to select what they believe to be the correct words that communicate their meaning or thoughts. Speak at a rate slow enough to allow understanding, without insulting the listener.

 #32 Speak with Normal Volume and Tone

For some reason, many Americans feel that if they raise their voice to someone who does not speak English well, that the person will understand what is being said. An excellent example is in the movie Rush

Hour with Chris Rock and Jackie Chan. In that movie, Chris Rock (who plays a police office from Los Angeles) goes to the airport to pick up a Chinese police officer (Jackie Chan). Rock assumes that Chan cannot speak English and raises his voice as he yells, "Do you understand the words that are coming out of my mouth?" Not only did Chan understand, he later begins to communicate fluently in English. When Rock acts surprised and miffed, Chan nonchalantly says, "I did not say I didn't speak English. You assumed that I did not speak English."

Such actions do little to enhance communication and learning. In fact, yelling or changing tone does nothing to enhance learner understanding and may well anger or embarrass them. It certainly makes you look foolish. Just because a participant is unable to speak English, does not mean that he or she is hearing impaired.

 #33 Paraphrase Messages

After focusing on what you think a participant says when they make a comment or ask a question, you should paraphrase what he or she said in your own words to ensure that your interpretation was correct. In cases where you did not understand correctly, paraphrase the part of the message to the point you did understand and then follow up with clarifying questions. For example, "Rasheed, I understand that your question concerns the differences between verbal and nonverbal communication, however, I'm not sure I understand your point. Specifically, what do you disagree with?"

 #34 Use Open-Ended Questions

Use open-ended questions to encourage participants to share information as opposed to closed-ended questions that do not allow you to accurately gauge a learner's viewpoint or understanding. Either because of embarrassment or to avoid saying "no," some participants from other cultures may not admit that they do not agree, have an answer, or want to do something when you asked with a closed-end question. This reluctance can lead to is understandings and possibly resentment if you do now recognize nonverbal signals being sent. Often someone will say that they understand when they do not. Many times they figure that they can get the answer from someone else later or that the meaning will come clear as the session or class moves forward and new information is presented.

 #35 Phrase Questions Carefully

Use simply phrased questions to stimulate communication, idea exchange, and enhanced learning opportunities. Ensure that your questions focus on a single issue instead of combining thoughts. For example, instead of asking a learner or the class, "What is the impact of the points we just discussed related to recent events in the community and how have you seen examples of this influence behavior among your peers?" try, "How have you seen what we just discussed affect people in this community?". In some cultures, questioning someone is considered intrusive and is therefore avoided. This is especially true if the questions involve personal information (e.g., "What was you childhood like in Viet Nam?").

 #36 Frequently Check for Understanding

Use short words and sentences when speaking. Frequently take the time to verify participant understanding of your message before continuing. Failure to do so might result in a waste of time and frustration for both you and your participant(s). To achieve this, avoid direct questions, such as "Do you understand?" Not only can this be answered with a yes or no, but it can also offend someone who speaks and understands English well. The nonverbal message is that the person may not be smart enough to get your meaning. Instead, try tie-in questions, such as, "How do you think you will do/use this?" or others that will give you an indication of whether there is comprehension of the information that has been provided. These types of questions help you and your participants to visualize how the information will be put to use. These questions will also give you a chance to clarify the information if the person has misunderstood your explanation.

 #37 Use Standard English

Avoid technical terms, contractions (e.g., don't, can't, wouldn't), slang (e.g., like, you know, out of sight,) or broken English (e.g., sentences which are imperfectly phrased or that fail to follow standard rules of grammar or syntax). Remember, if you are clear in your communication, some participants may understand English without being able to speak it perfectly or colloquially. In additional, some learners do not speak English because they are either self-conscious about their ability or choose not to.

 #38 Avoid Cultural References

To reduce the risk of misunderstandings by people who speak English as a second language, use universal language and references. Avoid words, examples, or acronyms that are unique to your culture. For example, U.S. trainers should avoid the following types of comments with participants who are not from the United States, "I'll need your 'John Hancock' on this form," (referring to a U.S. historical figure) "If plan A fails, we'll drop back and punt" (referring to U.S. football) "Looks like we scored a home run with that last activity" (referring to baseball) "Close, but no cigar" (referring to winning something at a carnival) or "Win one for the 'Gipper" (referring to Notre Dame football coach Knute Rockne). These phrases might be understood by someone acculturated to the U.S. society, but will probably not make sense to others. Such comments will only confuse your participants and do little to enhance comprehension.

 #39 Try Another Language or Use a Translator

Many countries encourage citizens to be multilingual and take language courses in school. If you speak a second language, try using it. Your non-English participants may understand. At the very least, they will appreciate your efforts. You might also ask if anyone else can speak the learner's native language and can help translate their intended message.

 #40 Be Conscious of Nonverbal Cues

Continually monitor nonverbal reactions as you converse with a participant. For example, people often have a puzzled or confused look on their face when they do not grasp a concept or something they heard. If you feel there is confusion or loss of comprehension, stop and try to reestablish a bond. Also, be aware of the nonverbal cues you send and make sure that they are in congruence (agree with) with your verbal message. For example, if you explain at the beginning of your class or training session that punctuality is important so that the program can stay on schedule, yet return late from breaks or restart the session late after lunch, you send a conflicting message. The potential problem this creates is that some learners will likely follow your lead and start returning late also.

 #41 Use a Step-By-Step Approach

When explaining something, clearly outline exactly what you will do or what will be expected of the participants. Write this information down for future reference by your learners so that you prevent misunderstandings. In taking this approach, you also aid the learners in your group who benefit from having information delivered visually better grasp concepts and instructions.

 #42 Keep Your Message Brief

Avoid lengthy explanations or details that might frustrate or confuse your learners. Use simple one-syllable words and short sentences. As mentioned earlier, such terminology is easier for someone to translate into their own language. Also, avoid being too brisk, or too simplistic in your explanations.

 #43 Avoid Sarcasm

Sarcasm do not work well in English, much less than in other languages. Sarcasm can lead to participant frustration, confusion, and embarrassment.

#44 Use Humor Cautiously

It is probably best to avoid jokes because cultural values and beliefs result in different levels of social acceptance on many topics. In addition, jokes are often based on incidents, people, or environmental factors from a specific culture. These might not be shared or understood by someone from outside that culture.

If you plan to use humor, make sure that the content or delivery will not inadvertently offend others. You are usually safest using self-effacing (directed at yourself) humor. Even so, be careful not to choose an aspect about yourself (e.g. body type, baldness, physical characteristics that stands out) that is shared by others or that can be viewed is a stereotype (e.g. all divorced people do . . . or all overweight people like me are too lazy to exercise) and that might embarrass a learner. If something is shared by someone in the class and they are self-conscious about the characteristic or aspect, they may feel that people are now looking at them as a result and may become irritated by your attempt at humor. They might then shut down and withdraw mentally or physically from the learning environment. Acceptable comments about yourself might involve something that you did that was foolish or was not well thought out and that caused you embarrassment or put you in a humorous predicament.

 #45 Avoid Criticism

Another other point to remember is that if you don't understand, or if participants make mistakes (e.g., they improperly fill out a form or use the wrong word), you should not point out the mistake, especially in public. Instead, take the responsibility for correcting the error or clarifying the misunderstanding (e.g. "I'm sorry I do not speak your language . . . ," "I am sorry that these forms are so confusing, I have trouble with them too," or "I do not know why this process has to be so difficult. I have trouble myself. I would like to go through it one more time. What do you think of that idea?").

 #46 Try Writing Your Message

Some participants understand written English better than the spoken word. If a learner seems to be having trouble understanding what you are saying, you may want to try printing your message legibly on a flip chart or providing a handout to see if such alternatives help. You may even try using recognizable symbols, if deemed appropriate (e.g., a stop sign when giving directions or a picture of an object if describing something) to communicate your message. If nothing else, a handout that participants can take home might be translated by someone else who can then explain it to the learner. Thus, learning ultimately takes place and the learner may be spared an embarrassing classroom situation.

CHAPTER 5

Participants
with Disabilities

B ecause there are so many different types of disabilities and each
person's disability affects him or her in potentially different
ways, it is impossible to list them all. In addition, many people have
invisible disabilities that affect their ability to function and create
learning challenges (e.g., diabetes, dyslexia, alcoholism, and cancer).
Such participants may not always be willing to disclose their disability and in some cases have learned to consciously mask them for
personal reasons. Respect their rights and desires and attempt to
provide a learning environment that is accessible to all participants.

When a disability is disclosed to you, accommodate the participant as much as possible. This is important because the Americans
with Disabilities Act of 1990, and other legislation in the United
States and in other countries, requires you to do so, but, more
importantly, because it is the correct thing to do. After all, isn't your
role as a trainer to facilitate learning? With a rising estimate of more
than 54 million people with some type of disability in the United

States alone, the chances of having at least one disabled participant in your session is very high.

The first step in creating a positive learning environment for people with disabilities is to ensure that your language, that of other trainers and participants, and your learning materials is not offensive or discriminatory. You read about this a bit in Chapter 1. If you cannot avoid referencing a person's disability, use the preferred language given in Table 2-1, *Referring to Participants with Disabilities*. The best approach is not to single anyone out for a disability or any other diversity factor. Simply address people by name or a generic term, such as man or woman. In additional, be particularly careful to avoid the potentially offensive word *handicapped*. Interestingly, this terms comes from old English, where it refers to a beggar or someone who traditionally was disabled and stood on corners with "cap in hand." If you must refer to someone with a disability, put the person before the disability.

Table 2-1 Referring to Participants Who Have Disabilities

Instead of	*Use . . . .*
Handicapped	Disabled or the specific disability
The deaf and dumb participant	The participant with a hearing and learning disability
Retarded participant	Participants with learning disabilities
Denise is a multiple sclerosis victim	Denise has multiple sclerosis
Ramone is confined to a wheelchair	Ramone uses a wheelchair
Genelle suffers from . . .	Genelle has . . .
Chris is a victim of . . .	Chris has . . .

GENERAL GUIDELINES FOR INTERACTING WITH LEARNERS WITH DISABILITIES

In addition to the specific suggestions offered in this section for interacting with learners with particular disabilities, here are some general strategies for success.

 #47 Be Prepared and Informed

You can locate large amounts of literature and information on disabilities. Take the time to read so you can appreciate the capabilities and needs of learners with disabilities. If you do train participants who use computers, there is a free video entitled *Enable* available on Microsoft's Internet website. The video provides raised awareness about the capabilities of people with various disabilities and how computers can help them compensate for lost abilities.

 #48 Don't Patronize

Participants with disabilities aren't your children; don't talk down to them. Just because they have a physical or mental disability does not mean they should be valued less as a learner or person. Allow all participants the same learning opportunities in your classroom.

 #49 Treat Them Equally

Just as you would other learners, work to discover their needs, then set about satisfying them. The key is to set up a learning environment in which all participants can get maximum benefit from the materials, information, and activities used. Ultimately, everyone should leave the classroom with enhanced knowledge and/or skills.

 #50 Offer Assistance; Do Not Rush
to Help Without Being Asking

Just as you would ask someone without a disability if you can assist them by moving a chair or carry a cup of coffee for them, you should do likewise for a person with a disability. Just do so in a manner that does not embarrass a learner.

Unsolicited assistance could be offensive, call undue attention to the person, and may even be dangerous if it is unexpected and causes the person to lose his or her balance.

 #51 Be Respectful

The amount of respect you show to all participants should be equally high and consistent. This includes tone of voice (showing patience), gestures, eye contact, and all the other communication techniques you have learned throughout this book.

INTERACTING WITH PARTICIPANTS
WHO HAVE HEARING DISABILITIES

Participants who have hearing impairments have special needs, but they also have certain abilities. Do not assume helplessness because someone is hearing impaired. In interactions with such participants, here are some things you can do to more effectively to assist learning:

■ Provide written information and instructions where appropriate and possible.

■ Use pictures, objects, diagrams, or other such items to communicate more clearly.

■ To get their attention, use nonverbal cues (e.g., waving or gesturing). Make sure that you have their attention before proceeding. One way to do this is to call their name and wait for them to respond verbally or non-verbally (by looking at you).

■ Use facial expressions and gestures to emphasize key words or convey thoughts.

■ Face the person directly and keep things away from the front of your mouth when speaking.

■ Enunciate your words and allow them to see your mouth form the words.

■ Use short sentences and words.

■ Check for understanding frequently through use of open-ended questions to which they must provide descriptive answers.

■ Communicate in a well-lighted room when possible so that they can see you.

■ Avoid backlighting that makes it more difficult to see clearly.

■ Reduce background noise, if possible.

■ Consider using someone who can communicate in American Sign Language to translate for learners with hearing impairments, if possible and appropriate (e.g. the learner understands and uses sign language.

INTERACTING WITH PARTICIPANTS WHO HAVE VISION DISABILITIES

According to the National Eye Institute in Bethesda, Maryland, approximately three million Americans have low vision, almost 1 million are "legally blind," and another 220,000 are totally blind. This means that if you stay involved with learners, your chances of encountering someone with a vision impairment are pretty good. Just as with persons who have hearing impairments, participants with a vision impairment may need special assistance, but they are not helpless. Depending on your session focus, you can assist your learners with vision disabilities.

One basic fact is that depending on the type of impairment, the person may have limited vision that can be maximized by certain actions on your part. Here are some strategies to use:

- Talk to a person with a visual impairment the same way you would anyone else.

- You do not have to raise your voice for the person to hear you better; the person is VISUALLY impaired. Do not change your vocabulary around them. It is okay to say things like, "Do you SEE my point?" or "Do you get the picture?"

- Speak directly to the participant and not to an interpreter (if they have one).

- If the learner uses a dog guide, do not pet, feed, or otherwise distract the animal without the owner's awareness and permission. A dog guide is specially trained to perform specific functions. If you interfere, you could confuse the dog, and this could result in an injury to the person.

- Speak to the person as he or she enters the room or approach the person so your location is known. Also, introduce others who are present or at least inform the participant of their presence.

- Ask how much sight he or she has and how you can best assist, if appropriate.

■ Find ways to paraphrase or repeat information if necessary, without sounding condescending or impatient.

■ Give very specific information and directions (e.g., "A chair is approximately ten feet ahead on your left").

■ If you are seating the person, face him or her away from bright lights that can obscure any limited vision he or she may have.

■ When guiding someone who is blind, offer your arm. Do not take the person's arm without permission because this could startle him or her or throw the person off balance. Let the person take your elbow and walk slightly behind you. Verbally communicate and guide them carefully.

■ When helping a person who is blind to a chair, guide his or her hand to the back of the chair. Also inform the person if the chair has arms to prevent him or her from being injured or overturning the chair by sitting on an arm.

■ Leave doors that are nearby and will be used either completely closed or open. Partially opened doors pose a danger to people with visual impairments.

■ Provide handouts with larger fonts, if necessary. Also, ensure that any computer monitors being used are adjusted to facilitate better viewing (e.g., contrast and color set appropriately and font size adjusted). Generally, someone who is sight impaired and uses a computer regularly can usually make his or her own adjustments.

INTERACTING WITH PARTICIPANTS WHO HAVE MOBILITY OR MOTION IMPAIRMENTS

Participants who have mobility or motion restrictions often use specially designed equipment and have had extensive rehabilitation involving the use of assistive devices that help compensate for the loss of the use of some part of their body. You can best assist them by offering to help, then following their lead or instructions. Do not make the assumption that they need your assistance, and then set about to do so. You can cause severe injury if you upset their balance or routine. Here are some strategies for better assisting these learners.

- Before a person who uses a walker, wheelchair, crutches or other device(s) arrives, do an environmental survey of the workplace. Note areas where spacing is inappropriate to allow mobility (a minimum of 36 inches is needed for a standard wheelchair) or where hazards exist. If you can correct the situation, do so. If not, make suggestions for improvements to the proper people in your organization. Remind them that the Americans with Disabilities Act and state regulations require an organization to accommodate these learners.

- Do not assume that someone who has such an impairment cannot perform certain tasks. As mentioned earlier, people who have disabilities are often given extensive training to learn how to overcome obstacles and perform various tasks in different ways. In many cases, they learn to be more efficient at a task than someone without an impairment.

- When displaying information or materials, ensure that you place them at a level where the person can see without undue strain (e.g., eye level for someone in a wheelchair so that he or she does not have to look up for long periods of time). An alternative is to provide the material in handouts.

- Stoop or sit to make direct eye contact with someone in a wheelchair so the person does not have to look up at an uncomfortable angle for extended periods. Do not push or lean on someone's wheelchair without his or her permission.

CHAPTER 6

Interacting with Different Generational Levels

In many cases, getting older often means being physically and mentally dependent on others. While this may be true on an individual basis, it is not due for the average older learner. The life expectancy and health of many people (at least in developed nations like the United States) has risen due to improvements in lifestyle and healthcare. For example, my 88-year-old mother lives with my wife and me and basically takes care of our house because she enjoys it. The woman is amazing as she regularly cleans windows, vacuums, dusts, washes and irons clothes and does pretty much whatever she feels like doing. Her memory is far better than mine. Such behavior and capabilities are typical of many people who are older than 50 today, which is why having an older learn in your classroom should not automatically be viewed as a challenge or difficult situation.

On the other end of the generational spectrum, many younger learners who attend classes come prepared with more knowledge of world events and the ability to do things technically that many trainers cannot do. This is because they have grown up surrounded by information access and technology. It is their way of life and often an expectation when they arrive at training or for a class. Failure to meet their expectations reduces their learning potential and can frustrate them. To improve your success in dealing with a variety of generational groups, plan ahead. By recognizing that each generation has its own values, beliefs, and concerns, you can start to identify ways in which you can relate to and involve each person in your session or class. The natural instinct for trainers and educators is to focus on the "norm" for his or her own generation and assume that others share those values or beliefs. This can lead to controversy and disagreements in class. To help overcome this tendency, consider creating a comparison chart of values that indicates what is important for each generational group so that you are prepared for issues that might arise. If appropriate, consider talking about values, shifts in cultural needs, significant world events or changes that have occurred during various eras, and demographics for different age groups in the class to raise awareness that participants have differing viewpoints and needs. In delivering training content, focus on what works and what does not work with each generation, but keep in mind that even within generational groups some learners will not "fit the mold." For this reason, be observant, listen, ask for opinions and do not stereotype anyone. Treat all learners as individuals and you will have great success.

One other thing to consider related to generational issues is that age is subjective to each individual. For example, there was a popular saying during the 1960s, "Don't trust anyone over the age of 30." This is because at that time, people of my generation considered 30 to be "old!"

MATURE PARTICIPANTS

Being older than you does not make a person or a learner less valuable or important. "Mature" is a term often to describe people over

Table 6-1 Generational Factors

By understanding how people of various generations view the world and events that they have experienced, you can often better tap into what motivates them and create a learning environment in which their individual needs can be met. The following partial lists can help you in this effort. Obviously, there are many other things that you might add to such a list if you want to discuss these with learners. Please note that the two columns are not correlated. For example, the "Stock Market Crash" does not equate to "Trust" (although it could impact trust of the government and financial institutions if someone lost a great deal of money when the event occurred).

Generational Defining Events/Changes	*Core Values*
WWII Generation (U.S.) (1920–1945)	
Stock market crash/Great Depression	Trust
Lindberg's first transatlantic flight	Dedication
Franklin D. Roosevelt elected/ New Deal	Honor/duty
	Play by the rules/formality
Social Security established	Respect for age/authority
Archduke Ferdinand assassinated	Fiscal conservatism
Pearl Harbor/World War II	Privacy
McCarthyism	Social order
Dust Storms	Hard work
Baby Boomer Generation (1946–1964)	
Korean War	Fitness/wellness
Rosa Parks protests discrimination	Hard work
Cold War	Political activism
Vietnam War and anti-war protests	Optimistic approach
Cuban Missile Crisis	Personal achievement
John F. Kennedy, Martin Luther King, Jr. and Robert Kennedy assassinated	Competitive
	Question authority
	Refuse status quo

continued

Table 6-1 (continued)

Generational Defining Events/Changes	Core Values
Civil Rights movement/Civil Rights Act passed First lunar landing Woodstock	Inclusiveness (e.g., age, race, sex, gender and teamwork) Time is money

Gen X (Nexters) Generation (1965–1976)

End of Vietnam War	Embrace technology
Sesame Street	Self-oriented/self-reliant
Watergate	Entrepreneurial
Energy crisis	Acceptance of diversity
Personal computer introduced	Living life to fullest
Three Mile Island meltdown	Independent/autonomous
Iranian Hostage situation	Nonconformity
AIDS/Drug abuse	Think outside the box
Rising Divorce/single-parent homes	Life balance important
President Ronald Reagan shot	Practical
Challenger shuttle disaster	Group-oriented
Stock market fluxuations	Fast-paced
Berlin Wall falls	
Operation Desert Storm	

Y Generation (1977–2000)

Oklahoma City Bombing	Realism
Proliferation of technology	Self-actualization
Multitasking in workplace	Weakened morality
Columbine High School massacre	Tolerant of diversity
Columbia shuttle disaster	Civic duty/activism
Drugs and gangs	Independent thinking
Hubble Telescope	Technically attuned
International Space Station	Confident
Y2K computer virus scare	Energetic

Table 6-1 (continued)

Generational Defining Events/Changes	Core Values
International terrorism/World Trade Center bombing	Fun loving
Iraq War	
Mars exploration	
Tsunami disaster	

the age of 50. For example, the American Association of Retired Persons (AARP) offers membership to anyone over the age of 50, AAA refers to older members as Mature Drivers and The Florida Safety Council (and many other safety councils around the country) has a Mature Driving Course for drivers who are 55 years or older. The point is that depending on your age, you may view people who are older as "old" or "mature" and should recognize and avoid any such bias or tendencies to do so in the classroom. Failure to do this could cause you to inadvertently single such people or groups out ignore or negate their contributions, or cause offense through words, actions or inactions. All of these possibilities could have a negative learning impact.

In fact, many mature participants are in excellent physical and mental shape, are still employed, and have more time to actively pursue personal and professional development activities than when they were younger. For example, as the *"baby boomer"* population (people born between 1946 and 1964) ages, there are more older learners than ever joining educational classroom and workplace training sessions. In additional, as the population ages, a greater need will exist for training and educational opportunities to retrain people and allow them to enjoy an extended quality-of-work life. Many people actually try new career opportunities as they become older. This often requires training to acquire new knowledge and skills. There are many examples of people from the pre-baby boom generation who have gone back to school to earn degrees and to learn new skills. To interact effectively with this population, consider the following strategies when training older learners.

 #52 Be Respectful

As with any learner, you should demonstrate respect. Otherwise, you may risk offending, alienating, or even angering these learners— in fact, it may have a negative impact on all participants. As in any situation, even if the participant seems a bit arrogant, disoriented, or disrespectful, maintain your professionalism. Recognize that sometimes their behaviors are a response to perceptions based on the verbal and nonverbal cues you send. When this happens, make a quick evaluation of your behavior and make adjustments, if necessary. If an older participant seems abrupt in his or her response, question whether you or someone else in the class might have nonverbally signaled impatience because of your perception that he or she was slow in acting or responding. Or, perhaps their age has nothing to do with their behavior. They may simply acting based on personality or preference. Your role as a facilitator of knowledge is to determine what prompted an action and take appropriate steps to respond.

 #53 Be Patient

Keep in mind that as some people age, their ability to process information and attention spans lessen. Do not assume this is true of all older participants, but be patient when it does occur. Allow older participants time to look, think, respond, react, or ask questions related to program material and concepts. Value their decisions and input. Another reason for their impatience might be that they perceive information being presented as too low level, that they already know it, or that the pace of delivery is too slow. Remember that many older learners view their time as money and have little patience for things that they do not perceive to be value added or from which they can draw immediate benefit. To avoid problems caused by such perceptions, keep your material and delivery style current, lively, and meaningful. Include specific tips for application of what is learned, give examples, use novelty and creativity to present the material, and involve learners by eliciting their needs and current knowledge. Let them be a vehicle for helping others learn as well and for providing resources to one another.

Regarding questions asked by learners remember that providing information effectively to all participants is crucial to enhanced learning. Even though you may have just explained something, listen to the questions, respond and reiterate, or restate, as necessary.

If It appears your message was misunderstood, try repeating the information, possibly using slightly different words. Another strategy is to gather opinions or invite response from other participants. Doing so potentially brings in additional views and information that helps answer a learners question or clears up a point that they did not clearly understand initially.

 #54 Be Careful Not to Sound Patronizing

If you appear to talk down to older learners, you could lose that participant, as well as others. Learners who are older should not be treated as senile! Patronization or a condescending attitude will cause any person, older or otherwise, to turn off or become offended. Such behavior can also reduce your professional image in the eyes of other learners.

 #55 Maintain a Degree of Formality

Addressing older learners in a disrespectful fashion (e.g., "What do you think about that young man?") can cause resentment and create a hostile environment. In many cultures, age and authority are revered. This belief should be recognized and respected.

If your goal is to set an informal environment, express that view at the beginning of the session, stress that learners should call you by your first name instead of Mr., Ms., professor, or whatever. In additional, let learners tell you how they prefer to be addressed. Ask them to write their name on a name tent as they wish to be called or addressed throughout the session. If they put Dr. or Ms, then respect that request and use the title when referring to or addressing the person.

 #56 Guard Against Biases

Be careful not to let biases about older people interfere with the way you interact with mature learners. Don't ignore or offend older participants by making statements (or allowing others in class to do so) such as, "Hang on, things have changed since you entered the workforce."

#57 Recognize Differences in Values

Each generation has concepts that it values or devalues. Do not let the values of your generation interfere with respect for and acknowledgment of differences when dealing with participants from other generations. This is important to the success of the learning experience for all participants and to help you maintain a professional image.

 #58 Use Their Knowledge

Because of their age, mature learners bring with them ideas, knowledge, skills, and experiences that you and many of your other participants do not possess. Use this as a resource. Incorporate opportunities where the mature learner can add input, offer guidance and coaching, give examples, and act as a cofacilitator, if appropriate. Getting experienced participants actively involved shows that you value what they have to offer and can actually enhance the learning experience for you and others.

 #59 Communicate Effectively

Even if someone does not exhibit common characteristics of hearing loss (e.g., incorrect responses, asking questions after you just gave similar information, facial expressions indicating she or he is straining to hear or may have missed the message), use the following to help enhance communication with all your learners:

■ Face the person directly

■ Talk slowly and enunciate words clearly

- Keep hands and objects away from your mouth

- Do not chew gum or eat food when talking

- Observe the learner's nonverbal cues

- Reword statements or ask questions again, if necessary

- Be positive, patient, and practice the good listening skills

- Stand near good lighting and minimal background noise, when possible

- If there is an impairment involved and an interpreter is with the learner, talk to the participant and not the interpreter. The interpreter will also hear and can react accordingly.

YOUNGER PARTICIPANTS

Like any other generational group, younger learners (25 and younger) come with their own values and beliefs. If they are from another ethnic group or minority, they also bring cultural differences. Sometimes referred to as the Gen Xers (1965–1976) and Y (1977–1995) generations, many younger learners come with their own generational values and beliefs. They are often categorized as selfish, unmotivated, and lacking goals, but this is not substantiated by research. Certainly, younger learners channel their energies differently from those before them, but this is not a bad thing. It simply means they are a product of their environment, the world as they know it, and they need and want to accomplish things important to them. This is no different from any generation in the past, and they should be valued for the views and ideas they bring to the learning environment.

STRATEGIES FOR INTERACTING WITH WORLD WAR II GENERATION LEARNERS

The following are some strategies that might help in incorporating various generational groups into the classroom or training experience.

 #60 Value Time Usage

Many people of this generation view "time as money" because of their experience with the depression and other geopolitical events of their era. For that reason, it is important that you plan effectively and schedule events in a logical sequence with a stated goal in mind. Don't waste their time, or let them feel as though their time is being wasted or they will likely turn off to learning and not return for training or other learning events.

 #61 Value Opinions

Because the members of the WWII generation have been through many hard times, some members of this group may adopt an attitude of "I earned it." They think that seniority and age should be respected. This can manifest itself in expecting others in the group to immediately go along with or share their opinions and ideas. For that reason, it is important that you give credit to thoughts they offer, then diplomatically elicit others ideas from the remaining participants and effectively integrate the ideas. You can often do the latter by stating, "John started us off with a great idea, and some of the things that the rest of you offered have added a bit more depth to it." This recognizes John as the catalyst and appreciates other contributions as well.

 #62 Listen to What Is Said

People from the WWII generation tend to stand by what they say is important to them. They grew up in a period where someone's word was his/her bond. Relationships and handshakes were more important than contracts and written documentation. While non-verbal communication is certainly an indicator of opinions or views, what someone says or does is traditionally more important for these participants and sends a more powerful and meaningful message. Make sure that you fully grasp opinions, ideas and concepts presented by these learners before responding in order to avoid confusion or a breakdown in communication or learning.

 #63 Allow Time for Assimilation

Traditionally, many members of the WWII generation are more silent and private in sharing opinions and views. To some extend this is a result of growing up in the McCarthyism era where the members of the government actively investigated and blacklisted or otherwise punished those viewed as unpatriotic or contrary to mainstream "American" thinking. In many cases, such people were actually labeled communists and ostracized by their peers and others. Before putting them in situations where they must contribute or offer input during training, provide opportunities for information to be shared and digested. Once members of the WWII generation have received enough data and have a level of trust with you and fellow learners, they typically can and will offer interesting perspectives.

STRATEGIES FOR INTERACTING WITH BABY BOOMER LEARNERS

 #64 Provide a Democratic Environment

It is important to speak with confidence in an assertive manner when dealing with participants from the baby boomer generation. Speak in an open, direct style, but avoid controlling language. As a whole members of this group are often competitive and do not trust authority and often challenge or debate "the establishment" (e.g., you, management, the educational institution, or human resources). If you seem hesitant or uncertain, you risk losing credibility and could have someone challenge you or even attempt to take control of the discussion or topic, especially, if they have expertise in a given area.

 #65 Be Prepared

Because of a generational history of challenging authority and political activism, you can expect that many boomers will have depth of knowledge and are willing to demonstrate it by challenging you. This can be helpful in expanding a conversation, but it can also get out of control if you waiver or have not done the necessary research and preparation to respond. Answer questions thoroughly and expect to be pressed for details. A good rule of thumb that I suggest when doing train-the-trainer or presentation skills programs, especially when dealing with baby boomer participants, is to have 7 to 8 hours of knowledge and be able to talk on a topic for every 1 hour you will present. This gives you the depth of knowledge needed to answer those "what if" questions that might be posed.

 #66 Communicate Using Body Language

Baby boomers come from the "show me" generation. As a result, they are sensitive to nonverbal cues and can be expected to draw strong opinions based on what they see. You should practice your presentation before the training session and be prepared to use congruent nonverbal and verbal cues so that your message is strongly stated and not misinterpreted. This will save you time explaining something that was misunderstood.

 #67 Be Open Minded

Because of the inquisitive and sometimes experimental (e.g. political issues and world events, drugs, and sex) era in which they were reared, many baby boomers have questions about virtually everything and are not hesitant to ask them. They also have formed strong opinions and views on most topics and continually ask "why" when asked to do something in a specified fashion. To demonstrate receptiveness and a lack of defensiveness when this occurs, present your opinions or comments in a way that demonstrates flexibility in your thinking and a willingness to consider alternative views or ideas. Also, be willing to modify an activity format if a more efficient or logical suggestion is made.

#68 Create a Cohesive
           Environment for Learning

Teamwork and inclusiveness are two important core values for many baby boomers. To enhance the learning experience and have the participants from this generation buy into your session, provide activities in which teamwork and inclusiveness play a major role. This is not to say that individual opportunities should not be provided, just make sure that you set up events that allow for sharing ideas, discussion and a chance to work with others.

STRATEGIES FOR INTERACTING WITH GEN-X AND GEN-Y LEARNERS

 #69 Deliver Information in
           an Active Format

Having grown up in a period when technology was coming into its own, many participants from this generation have short attention spans and need continuous stimulation. They are used to activity, playing video games, watching fast-paced movies, and hearing action-oriented commercials with tag lines, such as "when it absolutely positively must be there over night" and "just do it." To address this need, build in spontaneity, action, and a variety of stimulating activities when designing programs. Make your delivery upbeat and involve learners. Use a variety of media also. Change the pace of the program and your delivery at least every seven or eight minutes to keep Gen-Xers and Yers focused and interested. Also, talk in short "sound bites" to keep their attention. An example of the latter would be to provide a short bit of information then immediately ask questions related to how they would apply the concepts, so that they stay involved and mentally focused.

 #70 Communicate "with" Learners

Feeling in control and part of a process is important to many people from the Gen-X and Gen-Y. To help address this need, regularly ask learners for input and feedback while providing them with feedback on their performance. Share information with them about the process, next steps, and the value of using what they are learning throughout the session, so that they have a feeling of being "in the loop."

 #71 Make Learning Pertinent

Show Gen-Xers and Yers that what they are being asked to learn is immediately useful to them personally. Provide real-life examples of how they might use the information or skills in their personal and professional lives and how they can gain from doing so. It is very helpful if you can get someone from this generation to offer an example of a time when they did or used something related to the topic, and it added value. This helps validate information and concepts that you have presented.

 #72 Reduce Formality

Gen-Xers and Yers often take an informal approach to life. To tap into their thinking, keep sessions less structured from the standpoint of rules, regulations, systems, formal name usage, and other such techniques that tend to make training more "stuffy" and rigid. The use of props, games, contests, activities, and other strategies that make learning fun is appreciated, helps reinforce your message, and ensures that learning takes place. Group activities relate directly to their core values, so use them to integrate participants into the learning.

STRATEGIES FOR INTERACTING WITH Y GENERATION LEARNERS

 #73 Challenge Learners

As independent thinkers, many people from this generation like to look at options that are not consistent with mainstream thinking. They have learned through the use of technology that there are many possibilities in life, and they have seen phenomenal technical innovations (e.g., enhanced computer capabilities, special effects in movies, videogames that stretch the imagination and challenge abilities). To help capture and hold their interest, look for ways to incorporate innovation, technology, and problem-solving into your sessions. Use actions and words that challenge participants at every opportunity.

 #74 Respect Their Abilities

One challenge faced by many seasoned trainers is that they sometimes fail to value the knowledge, skills, abilities, and ideas of those less experienced learners. This is a huge mistake. While all learners may not address issues and situations from the same perspective, they all have something to offer. When presenting information or detailing activities, provide the tools and guidelines for successful completion and leave the "how" to learners. If you do this, learners are likely to be more energized and involved, and everyone in the room, including you, can potentially learn something new. The last thing that should happen is for X and Y generation participants to feel undervalued or talked down to. They will likely resent and rebel as a result of such actions on your part.

 #75 Continually Seek and Give Feedback

As with other learner groups, feedback is crucial for the successful outcome of any learning experience with the X and Y generation. Build time into your program for reflection and feedback from learners. Get their ideas, reactions, opinions, and questions. Make sure you also ask for their feedback on format, content, effectiveness of delivery, and any other element that will allow you to make adjustments during the session. It is not effective for you to wait until the end of the session to share feedback with participants. Make this happen periodically throughout the training or class.

 #76 Make Learning Fun

Learning does not have to be boring to be effective. As you create program content and materials, think of ways to make key points in an entertaining and stimulating manner. Use props, color, music, activity, food, or whatever you can think of to engage as many of the five senses as possible. Use inoffensive humor to create an upbeat atmosphere, but remember that anything you do should tie directly into program content and learning points. Do not do something simply to make people laugh. Learning time is too precious, and some people will be turned off by such activity. Still, do not take yourself too seriously. It is okay to take a light-hearted approach to most program content without losing your credibility or effectiveness.

 **#77** Encourage Risk Taking

Participants for the X and Y generation accept and appreciate realism and often enjoy trying things that "are on the edge." This likely explains the proliferation of the reality shows on television and the number of extreme sports that have emerged in the past decade. In your learning sessions, encourage people to take mental risks. Challenge them to think outside their paradigms and build in activities to teach them how to do so safely and within reason. Give them permission to break the rules and explore new ways of coming up with an answer and doing things.

CONCLUSION

No matter what generation of learners you have in your training sessions, the key is to treat them as **they** would like to be treated and to treat everyone equally. To do this, spend time before and during the session learning their needs, striving to meet those needs, and continually asking for feedback. Regularly monitor your effectiveness and make any modifications needed to better enhance the learning experience and help guarantee stated learning objectives. In part, you can accomplish this reading professional journals and articles, attending training classes that focus on enhanced learning, keeping up with advances in learning technology, and learning as much as possible about human behavior, cultural values and beliefs, and your topic(s). In addition, get and keep learners involved to help ensure transfer of learning and mental stimulation.

SECTION III
Personal, Behavioral, and Attitudinal Issues

There is no one correct way to handle every learner situation. Each person is different; each has personal experiences, ideas, needs, wants, and preferences. Your challenge as a trainer, facilitator, or educator is to try to identify the types of personalities you are dealing with and handle each situation that comes up on a case-by-case basis. The suggestions in the following section and others like it provide a point from which you can begin to deal with learners; however, this material provides only a guideline. You have to make an on-the-spot determination of what to do to create an effective learning environment and outcome. Use some of the concepts that you learned earlier, the additional ones presented below, and your own basic instincts. With these three elements, you will likely be successful in helping learners succeed.

CHAPTER 7

Poor Listeners

Participants come in all varieties related to their listening ability and skills. As you already read, you may be dealing with participants who are hearing impaired and not realize it. In these instances, the issue is not that they are inattentive or not listening, but that they simply cannot adequately receive verbal messages. For those people, use some of the techniques described in Chapter 5.

Unfortunately, many other learners do not have the skills to focus on verbal messages because they have never been formally trained how to listen effectively. Most public school systems in the United States do not teach listening as part of a learning curriculum to any major degree. For that reason, many participants lack the skills required to gather and process information through listening. Some researchers have found that the average adult in the workplace listens at approximately about a 25 percent efficiency level.[1] Thus without focused effort, they will miss approximately 75 percent of what is said! According to Andrew Wolvin and Carolyn Coakley, one survey found that three-fourths (74.3%) of 129 managers surveyed perceived themselves to be passive or detached listeners.[2] With these figures,

[1] Dr. Ralph C. Nichols, *"Listening Is a 10-Part Skill,"* Nation's Business, 45 (1957), p. 56.

[2] A. Wolvin and C. Coakley, *Listening,* 5th ed. Madison, WI: Brown & Benchmark, 1996, p.11.

Table 7-1 Listener Characteristics

Effective Listeners	Ineffective Listeners
Focused	Inattentive
Responsive	Uncaring
Alert	Distracted
Understanding	Unconcerned
Caring	Insensitive
Empathetic	Complacent
Non-emotional	Emotionally involved
Interested	Self-centered
Patient	Judgmental
Cautious	Haphazard
Open	Defensive

it is no wonder that listening is a challenge in the learning environment. Table 7-1 compares the characteristics of effective and ineffective listeners.

Much of our inability to listen effectively can be traced to early life experiences in which we were trained to listen (or actually, NOT to listen). Think of phrases your caregivers and others may have used to get you to listen. Some common ones are:

- Shut up and listen to me . . . . (often said in a harsh tone)
- Look at me when I'm talking to you! (again in a harsh tone)
- I'll talk; you listen.
- Silence is golden.
- Children should be seen and not heard.

While such statements are intended to help listeners focus on the message being delivered by not doing other things or making eye contact, they probably did not accomplish the intended goal because of the emotion involved. Would these phrases make you want to listen to someone if they were used toward you? Likely, they would do just the opposite, causing you to put up an emotional barrier and stop listening. That is probably what happened with your learners too as children. Thus, they did not positively learn many effective techniques that they need to communicate successfully today.

To help overcome some of these listening challenges in the learning environment, try the following strategies.

 #78 Prepare Your Learners to Listen

One of the simplest ways to help learners receive a message is to first get their attention. For example, if you are going to ask a question, call on a learner by name or the whole group as a whole, pause to be sure they heard and are attuned, and then ask your question (e.g. Class,[pause] what do you think would happen if . . . ?). While doing so, watch their nonverbal cues to ensure they do not seem confused and are getting the intended message.

 #79 Slow Down

The human brain is capable of comprehending messages delivered at rates of up 4 to 6 times faster than the speed at which the average adult in the United States speaks (approximately 125–150 words per minutes [wpm]). The difference between the two rates is referred to as lag time, or the listening gap, during which the mind is actually idle or distracted. The result is that the brain does other things to occupy itself (e.g. daydreaming). To prevent or reduce this distraction, you have to consciously speak at a pace that will focus your participants on key points and ask pertinent questions. Then, they are likely to respond more appropriately. In additional, provide handouts so that learners have a place to take notes. This not only helps them focus on and recall information, but it aids them later as reference material.

 #80 Vary Your Speaking Style

Any good presenter or actor knows the power of vocal variety. Techniques such as speeding up and slowing down, raising and lowering your volume, and incorporating pauses can all emphasize and punctuate your delivery. These strategies can also help focus or refocus attention when a learner is not listening or becomes distracted.

 #81 Chunk Information

Each day learners are bombarded with information from many sources. They get information in meetings, over the radio and on television, from customers and others, and in a variety of public locations. In many instances, they spend as much as five to six hours a day listening to customers, coworkers, family members, friends, and strangers. Such overloads can result in added stress, inadequate time to deal with individual situations, and reduced levels of effectiveness in the learning environment because they are thinking of other things.

Rather than add to this overload, create materials and deliver information in small chunks so that your learners can easily digest it. Present a maximum of 8–10 minutes of information and then have them process it individually or through a group activity. Give them only what they need for an activity, assignment, or to answer a question rather than telling everything that you know about a topic or issue. To reiterate what you say, provide written information to reinforce what was said. Bullet information verbally and in writing to make it quickly discernable and less confusing. This technique is especially helpful for visual learners.

 #82 Elicit Questions and Feedback

To determine if learners understand your information ask for feedback and provide numerous opportunities for questions and application of the material. As you read in earlier chapters, set up the expectation that they should ask questions early in your session. Let them know that there is no such thing as a stupid question and that they should feel free to ask questions or for clarification at any point. If they do not ask questions, have some prepared questions about program content that you use at various points in the program. This helps you gauge how well participants comprehend the content. It also provides an excellent review of key concepts covered.

 #83 Control Side Conversations

It is not possible for someone to focus on two activities simultaneously (e.g., talking and listening). Learners are also very distracted when peers are carrying on side conversations while you or a fellow participant is speaking. For these reasons, you should consider beginning your sessions by establishing ground rules, including one that specifies that only one person talks at a time. This can help you control some of these extra conversations. Post these guidelines on a sheet of flip chart paper on the wall for everyone to view and refer to it if someone violates one of them. Table 7-2 provides sample items that might go on guidelines for your session. It is often helpful to have learners create their own guidelines as a group at the beginning of a session. That way, the rules become their own and they are more likely to adhere to them.

Table 7-2 Sample Classroom Guidelines

Turn cell phones and beepers OFF (or on vibrate)

Focus on session content

Return from breaks on time

One personal at a time talks

Listen to others

No side conversations

Contribute candidly to discussions

Ask questions

Provide feedback to others

During the session, if you find that two or more people are having a separate conversation while other session-related activities are going on, casually walk towards them and close the physical distance between you and the offending learners. Make eye contact with them and smile as you continue to talk to the rest of the participants. Usually, this will signal them to stop talking and refocus. You may have to mention the posted guidelines in some extreme instances.

 #84 Review Frequently

Brain-based researchers have discovered that the brain is more likely to more effectively receive, retain, and act upon information received if the data is repeated in different ways and regularly. By creating games, reviews, activities, and other innovative ways of touching the five senses of learners, you can help ensure they get needed information and focus on it more effectively. In the case of poor listeners, you can increase the likelihood that they get a point by making it more than once using a variety of formats and approaches.

CHAPTER 8

Socializers

This type of learner is one who continuously holds side conversations in a low voice with those sitting nearby. When asked if he or she would share their comment with the rest of the group, the response is usually, "No" or "That's okay." To handle such participants, use one or more of the following strategies.

CONVERSATIONALISTS

 #85 Control Participant Behavior With Nonverbal Communication

Without drawing attention to the person verbally, move in their direction while continuing to talk to all participants. Position yourself near the person, possibly increasing your volume to draw attention to yourself.. Make direct eye contact with the person as your speak. The power of nonverbal communication (e.g., closing the distance, raising your voice, and making eye contact) is powerful and will normally say to the person, "Pay attention." Once the learner's attention is refocused, you can move back to the front of the room.

This technique works well in rooms configured for interaction, as outlined in Appendix C.

 #86 Divide and Conquer

A simple strategy that also ties to brain-based learning concepts is to move a person who is talking to another location or group. This is helpful for dividing small cliques of friends or coworkers who often sit together out of choice or a feeling of obligation. People who know one another are more likely to have side conversations, often about non-session related topics. To accomplish such movement, use one of the random techniques discussed in other parts of this book so that it is not obvious that you are doing so to relocate a talker. This can prevent the perception that you are singling one person out or picking on them. I often put extra grouping systems in place when planning a session even though I may not use them (e.g., colored dots on name tents, color-coded pencils, or whatever). Doing this allows me to arbitrarily group participants as needed based on the color of their name tent dot or type of pencil.

 #87 Query the Group

A more direct approach to handling a conversationalist is to ask a blanket question of the entire group and then directly call on the person talking to answer it (CPA questioning technique described earlier). For example, "Earlier, we discussed ___. Can someone give an example of how that would work in the workplace? *(Talker's Name)?*"

I generally reserve this strategy for learners who have been an ongoing nuisance and after I have tried other strategies, so that I do not embarrass anyone unduly. By the time I use this approach, other participants have started to show nonverbal displeasure with the conversationalist.

 #88 Appeal to the Talker Privately

When all else fails, you may need to either call a break or take the talker aside during a scheduled break. When you do so, be polite and tactful, but firm. Inform the learner that he or she is creating a diversion and try to determine if anything is wrong. Often a talker is just friendly and not aware of creating a distraction. Two possibilities for their actions might be that they did not volunteer to attend the session or are not feeling challenged by the strategies and techniques you are using. They may also feel that they already know what is being covered and are bored. The first possibility might need to be handled by asking the person to leave while the second could be dealt with by soliciting suggestions for making the material more meaningful to them.

CHAPTER 9

Monopolizers

This category includes participants who start talking in front of the group and do not want to stop. These learners are sometimes difficult to control because they are either extroverts who like personal interaction, enjoy being the center of attention, have many experiences that they want to share with others, or simply have poor communication skills and tend to ramble. Whatever the cause, such a participant can distract and ultimately annoy others while wasting valuable class time. If you do not control these talkers, you very likely will get off schedule and have trouble covering planned content. There are a variety of ways to address this second talker category.

 #89 Set Some Guidelines

If you plan to have someone speak to the group, set the criteria and a time limit. For example, if you want learners to introduce themselves at the beginning of a class, instead of saying, "Tell us about yourself and share anything you feel is important for others to know about you." Doing so basically turns the session over to the person until they decide to stop talking. This can be very time consuming and boring for other learners who probably really do not care about the person's background. Remember that they are there to learn something new and useful so you should not waste their time or yours. Instead of the above approach, try, "Take 30 seconds to introduce yourself and tell us one interesting thing about yourself that others should know."

 #90 Tactfully Interrupt

Once it becomes obvious that a participant likes to talk, use tactful interruptions to regain control. For example, while the participant is talking, politely interrupt and say something like, "That's an interesting point you just made. Let me stop you and get input from some others." Then, quickly call on another learner. If the talker seems to need other ideas or perspectives related to an issue being faced, you can offer to discuss during breaks.

 #91 Refocus Learner Attention

If the monopolizer tends to go off on tangents, especially by moving away from the original topic, interrupt with, "That sounds like it is important, however, we need to stay on topic. Can you and I discuss your point further at break?" The quickly start talking or call on someone else.

 #92 Control the Conversation

Use closed-ended questions to gain control of the conversation, then quickly ask someone else for input. For example, ask the talker "Does that happen often?" If he or she says yes, then quickly ask others for suggestions to offer the talker. If they say "not really" then state, "Well then, maybe we should spend our time more wisely on issues that do occur regularly." Then quickly proceed or ask others for input.

 ## #93 Remain Warm and Cordial, But Focused

Recognize that this person's personality is primarily one that causes the person to want to connect with others. Such people often get pleasure out of sharing information and developing relationships. To effectively deal with this type of behavior, smile, acknowledge comments, and respond briefly. For example, if the person comments that someone in class has a last name that is spelled exactly like his or her great aunt's and then asks where their family is from. After they get a response you could respond with *"Interesting how family names gets dispersed around the world."* You have allowed the monopolizer to get a response, but cut off a potential next question. Anything less would probably be viewed as rude from the participant's perspective. Anything more could invite additional discussion. Your next statement should then be topic related (e.g., "Let's get back to our session topic by examining . . . ").

 ## #94 Manage Your Conversation

Keep in mind that if you spend a lot of time with one learner, other participants may feel neglected. You can manage this situation by asking questions and making statements that let the monopolizer know that you must work with all participants and give them an opportunity to be involved and learn. In some cases a statement such as, "I know you said you have a lot of good ideas and want to share, however, you and others in the room will learn more if everyone has an opportunity to provide ideas and input. Thanks for your thoughts, now let's get some comments from others." Remember to focus on how your ending the interaction is to benefit *the participant* (e.g. the suggested statement above). Otherwise, he or she may feel put off and could either shut down or become a problematic learner.

Shy Participants

Opposite from the socializers and monopolizers are learners who do not want to respond in front of a large group. Because of personality issues, or perhaps a feeling that they do not know enough or have nothing valuable to contribute, these participants quietly melt into the group. They are attentive and proactive in capturing information, but quiet. By being alert to such behavior, you can possibly draw these learners into the program. Getting shy participants involved gives them a chance to learn and grow while providing additional perspectives and ideas to other learners. Many technically skilled people have introverted personalities, yet they obviously have much knowledge to share. To get shy learners involved, try one or more of the following strategies.

 **#95** Be Cordial

Smile, greet them by name, and use open body language to put them and others at ease. You also send a message of being approachable.

#96 Increase Their Comfort Level

Take time to get to know the shy learner at the beginning of the session or during breaks. Introduce him or her to other participants. If they feel comfortable around others or know them, chances are they will be more willing to interact or participate in the session. Ice-breaker activities can also help accomplish this.

 #97 Involve Them Gradually

You can start involving shy participants by asking them several easy closed-ended questions to which you are sure they have answers. This is an old sales technique. The idea is to ask a series of short answer questions that elicit positive responses or affirmative answers —and then ask for the sale. Psychologically, because the person has been talking for a while and agreeing with you, they often agree to the sale. If shy learners answer several easy questions, their confidence grows, and then you can ask them an open-ended opinion question (e.g., "How do you think that would work?" or "In what ways do you see that as being useful?").

 #98 Use Small Groups

You can use dyads (two people) and triads (three people) and small groups. Many shy people feel comfortable speaking in smaller group settings and interactions. Once they get comfortable in smaller settings and get to know other participants, they are more likely to open up during class discussions.

CHAPTER 11

Inconsiderate Participants

A study reported by the Associated Press in a number of newspapers in April 2002 found that many Americans admit to exhibiting rude behavior. Everything from failing to use the basics like "please" and "thank you" to cursing in public was reported. With such trends, it is no wonder that you will likely encounter participants who are inconsiderate or downright obnoxious. In the classroom, this pattern of negative behavior often manifests itself into two ways.

CATEGORY 1

This category of inconsiderate behavior includes participants who exhibit poor listening skills, interrupt others, call others rude names, point fingers, are loud, and demonstrate an arrogant approach when dealing with others. To deal with such individuals, you have a number of strategies to consider,

#99 Establish Ground Rules

At the beginning of your sessions, establish guidelines (as discussed in Chapter 7) for conducting the session (e.g., Only one person talks at a time; no interruptions; and raise a hand for recognition). Better yet, set aside time and have participants establish their own guidelines. This is helpful because they are less likely to violate rules that they generate them.

 #100 Remain Professional

Just because a participant is exhibiting inappropriate behavior does not justify your reacting in kind. Remain calm, assertive, and in control of the situation. For example, if you are talking to another learner and an inconsiderate participant barges in or cuts off your conversation, pause, make direct eye contact, smile, and firmly say, "*Please hold your thought for a minute while _____ finishes what she is saying.*" If the inconsiderate participant insists, simply repeat your comment and let the person know that if they remain patient you can finish your current conversation, then allow them to speak or share thoughts. By maintaining decorum in dealing with inconsiderate participants, you may be able to win the learner over or at least keep him or her in check.

 #101 Don't Revert to Retaliation or Try to "Show Them" Who Is in Control

Retaliation will likely only infuriate the learner, especially if you embarrass him or her in front of their peers. Remember that your objective is still to effect learning. If the inconsiderate participant or someone else perceives your actions as inappropriate, you could lose more than just the confrontation with the learner—you could lose others who are sympathetic to the participant.

CATEGORY 2

This second category of Inconsiderate participants includes those who fail to switch off cell phones and beepers or switch them to a vibrating setting. To deal with such individuals, consider the following strategies.

 #102 Set Guidelines Early

As part of your introductory remarks, ask participants to either turn all cell phones and beepers off or set them to vibrate and to let people in their office know that learners will check in during breaks. This can be part of a Training Agreement (see Appendix A) passed out and explained. In addition, request that learners not receive incoming messages from others outside the room unless they are on standby for an emergency. In such instances, especially if they receive more than one call, take them aside during a break and suggest they reschedule their training until a time when they are not on standby for an emergency. One technique for dealing with this problem is to put a note board outside the door for people to leave messages that can be retrieved by learners during breaks.

 #103 Allow Ample Breaks

In addition to requesting that cell phones and beepers be silenced, announce at the beginning of the session when breaks and lunch are scheduled so that learners are not watching the clock or arbitrarily taking breaks on their own. This will help learners mentally calculate when they can make and return calls or check messages and go to the restroom. Make sure that you stick to the announced schedule if at all possible, particularly the ending time, since participants will typically turn off mentally at the announced time anyhow.

 #104 Use Humor Where Appropriate

If someone's phone rings during the session, try something like, "*I know that is not for me, since I turned my phone/beeper off*" or "*If that is for me, I'm not here.*" After they respond to the ringing or beeping or return to the room, state to everyone, "*If you forgot to turn your phone or beepers off earlier, please do so now.*" Usually, this will embarrass the inconsiderate participant and prompt others to check to make sure they did not forget too.

 #105 Establish an Annoyance Fund

At the beginning of your session, when announcing session guidelines or rules, let everyone know that each time someone's phone or beeper sounds, they have to pay $1.00 (or have to perform some task). At the end of the session, you can hold a random drawing and give any collected money away. Those who paid into the Annoyance Fund are not eligible for the drawing.

 #106 Post "No Cell Phones/Beepers" Signs

You can add color and variety to your training environment by creating colorful flip chart pages or posters to hang around the room with messages like "No Cell Phones/Beepers" or "Quiet zone! Silence your technology". Additionally, you can do like many theatres now do and flash a humorous slide with clip art or a funny picture that reminds learners to turn off or silence their phones and beepers.

CHAPTER 12

Show-Offs

For a variety of reasons, some participants try to impress others with their knowledge or skills. Often, this is done through the use of complex multisyllable words, by quoting experts and information of which they are aware, or by dropping names of famous people whom they know or have met. Their behavior may be the result of a feeling of insecurity or a need to be recognized.

Perhaps they act out because of an underprivileged childhood environment that they have overcome as an adult and are now trying to flaunt. They may also believe that by using what they perceive to be an impressive vocabulary, reciting statistics, or demonstrating knowledge on a variety of topics, others will view them as more intelligent or competent. Whatever their motivation, they often alienate other learners while distracting from your planned learning objectives. There are a number of strategies for dealing with such participants.

 #107 Let Your Other Participants
Take Care of the Situation

Peer pressure can resolve many difficult participant situations. If the show-off is persistent, at some point others in the class will snicker, laugh, make side comments to one another, or outright tell the participant that he or she is wrong or that they do not agree. A key to successfully implementing this strategy is not to let the comments of others get out of hand. In addition, you should not appear to be taking sides. Your goal is to control the behavior of the show-off, not shut the person down or create a wasted learning experience for anyone. Many times, a show-off actually believes what he is she is are saying is contributing value to the conversation. In many instances, this is true or important. It is their approach that irritates or frustrates others and that needs to be channeled effectively.

 #108 Get the Opinion of Other Learners

If a show-off continues to share opinions or views in a pompous manner, state "That is an interesting perspective. Let's hear from some other participants." Then, immediately put the question or comment out for group discussion or response.

 #109 Use Body Language
to Your Advantage

Body language is a powerful classroom management tool. You can often control the amount of access that the show-off gets to the group by physically turning away from the learner. Additionally, as he or she speaks, reduce the amount of encouraging behavior you use (e.g., smiling, open body language, nodding, and using verbal enablers like, "Uh huh" or "I see"). Instead try arms crossed, expressionless looks, and verbal sounds like, "Hummm." This "cold shoulder" approach, coupled with some of the other strategies listed in this chapter can potentially help eliminate or control the show-off's behavior.

 #110 Use Small Group Activities

By forming small groups and randomly selecting group leaders (see the suggested techniques for doing this in Appendix D and E), you limit the Show Off's access to the larger group. This can sometimes help because in smaller groups, many participants will be more assertive and willing to speak up to preempt the Show-off or to put pressure on him or her to be quiet.

 #111 Ignore the Show-Off

If the participant raises a hand to comment or respond to everything you say or ask, ignore the hand and call on someone else. If the show-off then interrupts to offer an opinion, use an approach similar to Strategy #110 and state, "Let's hear from some other people on this. You've given us quite a bit already."

 #112 Speak With the Show-Off
During a Break

As soon as possible, take the show-off aside and suggest that while he or she appears to have a lot of interest and knowledge or may be a smart person, others may shut down and not participate if not given the opportunity. Ask the show-off to save some comments and allow others to share their perspectives. Often, this will prompt a defensive reaction of, "Well, if you don't want me to comment, I'll shut up." If this occurs, reinforce the value of the show-off's knowledge, but ask that remarks be limited or kept simple so that others can learn through their own participation. Remember that the show-off is also there to learn.

CHAPTER 13

Experts

Another category of difficult learners are those who have (or think they have) a lot of subject knowledge and skill. This know-it-all group can cause potential problems or confrontations if handled incorrectly. They are often people who are technically skilled, knowledgeable, and well trained or educated.

Many of these people are confident and have a need to be heard. They will often challenge what the leader says or give additional information following each point because they want to show their knowledge. This is the reason why you should not put yourself in a position where you arbitrarily say, "research shows . . . ." An expert will likely ask for a source, thus putting you on the defensive or damaging your credibility if you cannot provide one. If an expert says something like "research has found . . . ," say something like, "That is interesting, I've never heard that (assuming that you have not). What is the source so we can all go back and look it up to learn more? Typically, they will not know and you have in effect placed their credibility in doubt with others. Here are some other ideas for handling this type of learner.

#113 Use Subtle Pressure

Be polite and do not show signs of irritation when an expert speaks up. Listen to what he or she has to say, then defer to other learners (e.g., "How does that sound to the rest of you?"), rather than confronting the expert or disagreeing. Let other participants potentially disagree. This peer pressure can soften the expert's approach. You can always add more information following what is offered by other learners, or you can cite expert sources. If the expert challenges dates, credibility of sources, or whatever, simply state, "I wasn't aware of that. I'll research it and get back to you." You can then state, "Let's get back to our topic" and move on. Obviously you should not use this later approach often because others may begin to see the expert as more knowledgeable and start deferring to what he or she says rather than what you are providing. This is why having at least 7–8 hours of topic knowledge that you read about earlier comes in handy.

 #114 Acknowledge Their Expertise

Identify any experts in your group through a pre-session needs assessment or a quick in-class assessment once everyone arrives. Introduce yourself to them before the session begins, if possible, and ask if they would mind you calling on them for additional input from time to time. Most experts will be flattered and agree. Once the session starts, acknowledge their presence or expertise. This stroking of ego can help defuse their need to try to take control. You might also make such a person a small group leader during an activity. However, be careful to monitor them in group sessions. Otherwise you may find all other participants deferring to this person's knowledge or experience when they are supposed to brainstorm or come to group consensus. If this seems to be happening, take the expert aside and again appeal to his or her knowledge by encouraging the expert to guide the thinking of others rather than providing all the answers. By being professional and partnering with experts, there is normally little problem having them in a session.

 **#115** Do Not Put Experts on the Spot

Just because someone has been identified as having an area of expertise or job skills does not mean that he or she has knowledge on every related aspect of the topic or field. It is okay to elicit ideas or suggestions from Experts (e.g. "*Expert,* do you have anything else you can add to that last comment?"). This is a better approach than saying something like "*Expert,* why don't you respond to Ellen's question about . . . "). This latter approach potentially puts the Expert in the awkward position of not having knowledge of the issue and could inadvertently embarrass or alienate him or her. This actually happened to me recently in a Master's level course that I was taking. Since I am also an adjunct instructor at Webster University the instructor knew that I am a published author. Someone asked the difference between an Abstract and an Executive Summary. The instructor turned to me and said, "Bob, you are a published author and can probably answer that better than I can. Will you explain the difference?" Luckily I did know the difference and was able to respond but it could have been embarrassing for both of us.

CHAPTER 14

Agitators

Some learners have personalities and behavior patterns that are constant irritants to others. If you are unfortunate enough to have such a person in your session, your patience will be tested, as will that of the other participants. The reasons for such behavior vary, but experience seems to indicate that these people are inwardly insecure and feel a need to demand attention in whatever way and form possible. Most likely, such people have been rebels all their lives. They have probably resisted authority in many forms, so you are not likely to succeed in appealing to their better side or winning them over.

You probably represent the organization or management to them, especially if you work for or were brought in by the Human Resources department, upper management, or the administration. As such, you are fair game since they probably would not likely take pot shots at HR or upper management representatives directly. The following strategies might help in dealing with agitators.

 #116 Maintain Control

Be firm and polite, but take charge of the situation immediately. Other participants look to you to intercede, especially if the agitator is attacking one of them or their ideas. In a cordial manner react to a negative or sarcastic comment with, "That may be how you feel — _____, however, we should hear from others about their views." Then call on someone else immediately. Do not let the agitator corner you into a one-on-one confrontation. Others who are friends of the person may side with him or her.

#117 Partner With the Person

Partner with the agitator to diffuse his or her argument and thereby regain control of the session. Look for something in what the person says with which you can agree. For example, if an agitator says something like, "You stand up there and give us all these great ideas without ever having worked in this organization (or as a _____)," you may counter by agreeing, "You are correct. I have not worked in this organization (or as a _____), however, I have held similar positions in other organizations, have done research on the issues you brought up, or spoke with a number of employees with this organization before the session to gather background information. These strategies have worked in similar situations and this program's content is based on my experience and findings." This is all assuming you have done these things. Do not lead the agitator or any other participant into believing you have done something that you have not. If caught in a lie you can lose and never regain credibility with them and other learners.

#118 Agree With the Agitator

Simply agree with the agitator and ask if anyone else has a comment, then move on. Do this only if what they have said is true or accurate.

#119 Agree to Disagree

State, "We seem to have differing opinions on the issue. Can we simply agree to disagree and move on? You and I can discuss it further during a break if you would like."

 #120 Ask The to Leave

If the situation becomes intolerable or counter-productive, call a break, take the Agitator to a private location, explain the problem he or she has created, and ask him or her to leave. If appropriate, notify their supervisor or other appropriate person of what happened as soon as possible. In many cases, their behavior will not come as a surprise since they likely act this way in other environments and with other people. A key concern in dealing with a person in such as situation is to be tactful and professional, while remaining alert for signs of potential violence (see Appendix F for signs and strategies for dealing with potentially violent learners).

Revolutionaries

Some learners come to a session with their own agendas. Although you may have clearly stated the program objectives and given an accurate description of content in promotional material, they want something else and attempt to take over or dominate. As a result, they try to take control of the session by stating, "What we really need is . . . (and go off on a tangent)."

To deal with such learners, try some of the following strategies.

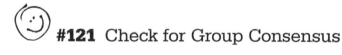 **#121** Check for Group Consensus

Do a quick in-class needs assessment through either a show of hands or an anonymous questionnaire. Ask, "Who agrees with _____ ?" If a majority of participants feel the issue is important, you may want to do a quick content adjustment and build it into your program. You can do so by either modifying and shortening other less important topics or replacing something altogether. Obviously, to do this you need a strong subject knowledge base and have confidence in your ability to think on your feet. One way to accomplish the inclusion of unplanned agenda items is to have small group brainstorming on the issue. Next, have the small groups brainstorm possible solutions.

In such situations, a contributing cause for some participants' need to address other issues is that they never have the time or opportunity to do so during their regular day. The only time they all come together is in training or other sponsored events. They likely know the problems and probably have good ideas for solving them, but they need a forum to put it all together. When this type of issue surfaces, you may deal with it in the above manner. Traditionally, I get my highest session evaluation marks for providing valuable tools they can use. In reality, all I did was get out of the way and facilitate their problem solving.

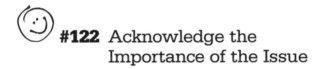 **#122** Acknowledge the Importance of the Issue

Let revolutionaries know that while the issues being raised are important, the group needs to get through the session content first. Tell them that if time exists at the end of the program, these other issues can be addressed. Capture the idea and any others that surface on a posted flip chart page to make it visual, to show its importance, and to remind you of it later. Some trainers call such a page a "Parking Lot" of ideas or issues and even do colorful graphics to make the sheet look like a parking lot. If time does not exist at the end of the session, offer to discuss it with the revolutionaries after the program. If others agree that it is an important issue affecting them all, either try to get an additional session scheduled to address it or pass it along to management with the recommendation that action needs to be taken.

CHAPTER 16

Pessimists

S ome participants, for a variety of reasons, will try to squelch the ideas of others. These are the learners who, no matter what is offered, automatically respond, "Yes, but . . . ." My personal belief is that this behavior is learned from caregivers. Likely, their role models were poor communicators who failed to give enough positive feedback or reinforcement or did not take time to explain "why" about various things. Typically, pessimists will use phrases such as:

We tried that before and it did not work

Sounds good in theory, but it won't work here

That will never work in the real world

Upper management (supervisors) will not support that

Policy (law/regulations) prevent us from . . .

We don't have time/money/resources to . . .

The following strategies can help in dealing with pessimistic learners.

123 Try to Understand Their Logic

Ask for the person's reasoning as to why an idea will not work and then put the topic out to the group for input or feedback on what the pessimist said. Ask, "What do the rest of you think about what _____ just said?" Be careful and prepared for what you will do if they agree with the pessimist. Sometimes, there are real unspoken issues that you are not made aware of that prevent application of training concepts. If important issues surface, you may want to either flip chart them for later discussion, give them to management (assuming learners agree), or take a diversion and discuss the issue, then brainstorm possible courses of action for a short period of time. Otherwise, learners may be distracted by the issue and you will end up with a bunch of socializers on your hands. If others do not agree with the pessimist, they will likely wear that person down. Peer pressure is a powerful tool for quieting dissention.

 #124 Give Them the Benefit of the Doubt

Assume that the pessimistic learner may have a good point and ask, "What alternate ideas do you have?" or "What do you suggest instead?" Often they will not have given any real thought to the issue and cannot think of another option. If that is the case, suggest that the group discuss the original idea presented further and that if the pessimist thinks of something later that you are willing to consider it. On the other hand, if the pessimist does have an alternate suggestion, listen to it, then discuss the merits as a class or take other action deemed appropriate.

CHAPTER 17

Autocratic or Controlling Participants

B ased on the situation, some participants can be demanding for a number of reasons. Many times domineering behavior is part of a personality style or personal background. For example, it could be a reaction to past learning encounters. A demanding learner may feel a need to be or stay in control, especially if he or she felt out of control in the past. Some of the factors that contribute to such behavior include:

- Children without siblings who are used to being the center of attention;

- Insecure individuals needing a lot of attention;

- Type "A" (driven, goal-oriented people) who are very competitive and have a need to be involved;

- Former military leaders or managers used to being assertive, taking initiative, and acting as a catalyst for action;

- People who have an underlying agenda when attending a session (e.g., they were told to attend, have already attended

similar programs in the past, or do not support you or the
training and do not see its value);

■ Angry learners who have a grudge against someone else
and transfer their frustration to you and other learners. For
example, they might work for a supervisor who controls
employee behavior tightly and sent the autocratic participant to training as a punishment for performance problems.
Because the learner cannot act out against the supervisor,
their anger is transferred to you and your session because
you represent the organization.

Whatever motivation the autocratic learner has, the behavior ex-
hibited can have a negative impact on you and other learners.
Because of this, you must assertively (not aggressively) address it.
The following strategies might help.

#125 Establish or Use Training Agreements

You can develop session guidelines or "ground rules" related to roles
and expectations for yourself and participants before a session
starts or as part of your program (see Appendix A). An alternative
is to involve participants in the development of guidelines as part
of your opening remarks. To do this, pass out 3 × 5 cards and ask
learners to write down one guideline they think is necessary for a
successful learning environment. Give an example to get them started
(e.g., Respect opinions of others, Do not interrupt, or Return from
breaks on time). Next, form several equal-sized small groups and
have participants compile what they wrote on the 3 × 5 cards onto
a flip chart page. Once all groups are done, have a spokesperson for
each group share the list while you or someone else compiles a list
on a single sheet. Post this list on the wall throughout the session

for reference. Stress that all learners should abide by the rules that they created and award small prizes (e.g., candy, stickers, or other similar incentives) throughout the session to those who do adhere to the tenets. Whenever someone violates the rules, point to the guidelines and remind them to comply with "their rules."

 #126 Befriend the Autocratic Learner

Psychologically, if you partner with learners, they are often less likely to create challenges during training. A simple way to accomplish this is to warmly greet all participants by name as they arrive. Introduce yourself and shake hands with them. The act of physically coming into contact with learners helps form a subconscious bond of "friendship." Friends are less likely to attack or cause problems for people with whom they have bonded. Law enforcement officers, salespeople, and other professionals have used this approach to effectively build rapport for years.

 #127 Monitor Overbearing Behavior

One of your important facilitative roles is to protect learners from those who attempt to abuse, dominate, and control. Your participants will expect you to fulfill this role for orderly learning to occur. Failure to do so can lead to frustration, anger, and diminished transfer of knowledge and skills.

During your sessions, you must observe and control behaviors that are overzealous, rude, domineering, or otherwise offensive. This is important regardless of the size of the group. When using this technique, visit each group frequently to ensure involvement by all group members and that no one person is controlling the discussion.

Look for signs of dominance (e.g., the autocratic person standing and looking down on the group, a raised level of volume from the autocrat, other participants seemingly being disinterested and the autocrat dominating the conversation). If you note such behavior, intervene to redirect discussions and regain control of the group. Once this is done, appoint a person, other than the autocrat to lead and keep the group on task.

 #128 Incorporate Small Group Activities

When designing your session content and delivery format, build in a variety of small group activities. By continually changing the format and pace of your session, you better limit access and opportunity to the autocratic participant. Members of a small group can often exert pressure on someone who attempts to dominate or control.

 #129 Creatively Assign Volunteers

Use some of the ideas found in the Appendices (e.g., Appendix E) to randomly select small group leaders and scribes. By using such techniques, you can continually rotate responsibility and encourage a wider range of involvement by more learners. This limits the opportunities that an autocratic participant has to lead and control.

 #130 Use Rewards and Recognition

By applying some basic concepts of human motivation (Appendix B), you can often influence learner behavior and encourage involvement.

As learners offer ideas, respond to questions, assist with tasks, or otherwise participate, give them tangible rewards (e.g., candy, toys, gifts, or other similar inexpensive items). You can also either recognize their behavior in front of the group, or individually, and thank them for playing an active role. By doing these simple things, you can reduce the opportunities for the autocratic participants as other learners become actively involved.

#131 Be Professional

A learner's unprofessional behavior does not justify similar behavior from you. Do not raise your voice or verbally retaliate. This may only cause the participant to revert to past negative learned behavior. Remember when someone called you a name as a child and you retaliated by responding by yelling back. Soon voices raised, and possibly shoving started. This is how we learn behavior that we often repeat as adults. The outcome of such an episode is that you, the participant, and other learners in the session lose as the problem escalates.

#132 Handle the Autocratic Participant With Respect

Showing respect does not mean that you have to accommodate every idea or objection that a participant has. It does mean that you should make positive eye contact (not glaring), remain calm, use his or her name, and let the learner know that while input and discussion are welcome, it needs to be productive and appropriate. The participant also needs to recognize that there are others in the room who have valuable insights and thoughts that should be heard. Work positively toward resolution of the issue.

#133 Be Firm and Fair While Focusing on the Participant's Behavior

Assertive behavior, is an appropriate response to a domineering or demanding participant; aggression is not. In addition, remember the importance of treating each learner as an individual.

#134 Tell Autocratic Participants What You Can Do, Rather Than What You Cannot Do

Do not focus on negatives or what cannot be done when dealing with your learners. Stick with what is possible and what you are willing to do. Be flexible and willing to listen to ideas, criticism, or requests. If something suggested is possible and will aid learning, compliment the person on the idea (e.g., "Stephanie, that's a good suggestion, and one that I think will work"), then try to make it happen. Doing this will show that you are receptive to other ideas, are truly working to assist in meeting your learner's needs and expectations, and that you value the opinions of others.

In addition, remember that if you can psychologically partner with the learner, they are less likely to attack you or your ideas. Be sure that your willingness to assist and comply is not seen as giving in or backing down. If it is, the participant may make additional un-realistic suggestions or demands. To avoid this you could add to the earlier example by saying something like, "Stephanie, that's a good suggestion, and while we cannot do this right now, I think that your suggestion is one that we need to address later, if time permits. If not, I'll pass it along to management for consideration, or to use as a basis for future training." This puts the learner on alert that while an idea may not be adopted right away it might be used later.

 #135 Use Controlling Body Language

As you read in other sections, nonverbal cues can be used to send powerful messages. There are a number of cues that can be used to reduce the effectiveness of an autocratic participant.

- **Eye Contact** can be used to acknowledge or ignore an autocratic learner. When the participant is attempting to gain attention through dominant behavior, make eye contact with another participant and open a dialog while ignoring the autocratic participant. In situations where the autocratic participant has a raised hand to respond to a question or to attract your attention, you might make eye contact and say, "*(Autocratic Learner),* you have had a number of opportunities to give input, let's give someone else a chance," then, call on someone else without hesitating.

- **Closing the distance** by moving nearer to an autocratic participants while making eye contact with him or her can signal that you want to regain control. By moving closer to someone, you effectively invade his or her personal space and can signal disapproval. In additional, you can block an autocrat's access to other learners by positioning yourself in front of the person and facing away from them while standing between them and other participants.

When an autocratic participant dominates the dialog in a small group, you can approach the group, position yourself near the domineering learner, and squat down to eye level. Once in this position, make eye contact and then open a dialog with the entire group. Call on individuals other than the autocratic learner. In effect, you can shut out the dominant person. You might also ask questions of various group members to get their input.

 #136 Discuss Their Behavior with Them

If the autocrat's behavior is disrupting learning or planned activities, as a last resort, call a break or take the person aside during a scheduled break. Explain the importance of gaining input from all learners, let the person know that this behavior (whether conscious or unconscious) seems to be impacting others and ask him or her to be less forceful. Let this person know that such behavior can inadvertantly give others the wrong impression.

CHAPTER 18

Clowns

In many groups, you will encounter one or more people who are fun loving and seek attention through practical jokes or humorous words or actions. While such behavior can help liven a session, it can also distract if carried to an extreme. It can be compounded when friends of the clown continue to encourage the behavior or contribute their own. As with any other type of behavior described in this book, before fixing blame for the behavior on learners, ask yourself if there is something that you are doing or not doing that is contributing to the learner's behavior. If there is, correct it right away.

To address clowns, try the following strategies.

#137 Ignore the Behavior

Ignore the behavior or comments if possible. This eliminates any psychological reward in the form of the person being recognized before the group. People who use humor to get attention in public settings often have learned that behavior as children. To get the attention of parents and others, they likely acted out in humorous ways as children.

#138 Used Timed Activities

If someone's clowning around is wasting time or affecting the learning schedule, use small group activities. Assign specific tasks to individuals or groups and give specific time limits. You might even make the clown a group leader so that he or she feels pressure to have the group finish on time. Announcing that rewards for punctuality will be given can add additional incentive to stay on task.

 #139 Appeal to the Learner

Appeal to the learner's serious side by asking session-related questions or opinions of them. Many times a humorist is attempting to make a point or express an opinion in a roundabout funny manner.

 #140 Separate Disruptive Participants

If friends in a small group are contributing to and encouraging the behavior, separate them in a random manner. Use some of the techniques described the Appendix D.

 #141 Discuss the Behavior Privately

If the clown's behavior is really a problem, call a short break, meet with the clown, and discuss the need to remain on task.

CHAPTER 19

Distant or
Distracted Participants

M any things occupy the minds of your learners in today's world. They are bombarded with information, asked to "do more with less" in the workplace, have to content with rising costs, downsizing, and a world filled with drugs, terrorists, and uncertain economics. Compound all of this with personal issues related to grades, finance, health, and family, and it is no wonder that many participants show up for training or class and have trouble staying focused.

Another potentially distracting element is that learners are often attending sessions because they are required to do so. In the workplace, employees are not consulted before being registered. Often this is done as a last effort before termination because they are not performing up to standards (many times, due to poor coaching or supervision on the part of their manager because they do not have the skills or desire to effectively assume these roles). Considering these things, it is easy to see how someone might not be motivated to focus on learning or might have other things on his or her mind.

Generally, the following are several categories of distracters that can cause problems for other participants and some strategies for handling them.

PERSONAL OBSTACLES

Internal personal issues can sometimes create unconscious barriers for learners which can affect their ability to focus and interact effectively in a learning environment. The following are some obstacles along with suggestions for dealing with them as a trainer or educator.

Biases

Biases are opinions or beliefs about a specific person, group, situation, or issue that can cloud someone's ability to objectively listen to what is being said. These biases may result in preconceived and sometimes incorrect assumptions. They can also lead to a breakdown in communication and attention. In a training environment, a learner may have biases or disagree with points being made, a facilitator, the venue, or any number of things that could distract from learning. The following strategy may assist in overcoming or at least subdue learner biases.

 #142 Help Raise Awareness of Personal Values

If someone is distracted by others in the group, an issue, or a situation related to the training (e.g., someone perceives that you are playing favorites or giving special treatment to others), you need to identify and try to remedy what is bothering the learner. Depending on the issue, you may want to address the fact that everyone is equal in the class and all have the same opportunities to participate. In addition, encourage equal participation actively by calling on all learners occasionally and providing opportunities for various people to get involved or take leadership roles. If necessary, you may have to take a learner aside to counsel him or her if their actions or comments become distracting or disruptive. There is no room in training for prejudice or biases. Encourage everyone to be accepting and keep an open mind throughout training.

Psychological Problems

A participant's psychological state can sometimes impede effective learning and attention. If a participant is angry, upset, or simply doesn't want to deal with a particular person or issue, their focus may be negatively affected. Therefore, try the following strategy.

 #143 Identify and Help Diffuse Emotion

Before people can focus on learning, they need to get past any emotional roadblocks. If you notice that someone seems to be distraught or emotionally distracted, take them aside during the break to ascertain what is causing the situation. Make sure that it is not something that you or other participants have done. If you determine it was caused by something in the session, take immediate action to remedy the situation and apologize to the learner. If the problem is caused by outside factors, suggest that if the learner cannot get past it and focus on the session, it might be best for them to take care of what is bothering them and return for another session date. If is a work-related situation, suggest that they speak with a supervisor or seek help from the organization's Employee Assistance Program (EAP) if one exists. If you are in an educational environment suggest that the learner visit a counselor, if one is available.

Physical Conditions

Other internal factors that contribute to or detract from a learner's attention are wellness and fitness. When someone is ill, fatigued, in poor physical condition, or just not feeling well, mental focus can suffer. When someone is tired and not alert, the brain starts to wander or get off task. Such a person needs to be engaged.

 #144 Increase Movement

Get participants up and moving with simple stretching activities or cross-lateral activities (where they pull from both sides of their brains to make them more alert). To do this, have everyone stand and participate in some simple movements where they are told to use one side of the body to reach the opposite side. For example, "reach behind your head with your right hand and pat yourself on the left shoulder," or "raise your left foot behind the right knee and pat the heal of your foot with the right hand four times." Such activity, which requires learners to stop and think, engages their brains and bodies, thus getting blood flowing to the brain to increase alertness. It also provides a novel change of pace and a bit of humor to the program.

BUILD IN ACTIVITIES

Another way to stimulate learners and their brains is to build in icebreakers ("get acquainted" activities), small group discussions, role plays, simulations, games, and other activities in which learners physically change locations and pace. Such activities can be used to present concepts, encourage thinking, review material, and engage learners physically and mentally.

Circadian Rhythm

Everyone has an internal "clock" cycle. This is the natural 24-hour biological pattern by which they function. This "clock" often identifies the body's peak performance periods. People said to be morning people typically perform best early in the day. They often wake early, "hit the ground running," and continue until after lunch, when the natural rhythm or energy level in their bodies begins to slow down. For such people afternoons are often a struggle. They may not do their best thinking or perform physically at peak by that point in the day. Evening *people* have the opposite pattern of energy. They struggle to get up or perform in early morning; however, in afternoon and evening they are just hitting their stride. They often stay awake and work or play until the early hours of the next day when the morning people have been sound asleep for hours. From a listening and learning standpoint, it is important to recognize your own natural body pattern so that you can position your heaviest amount of important listening or productivity during your peak period if possible.

 #145 Plan Around Peak Periods

Ideally, training will be planned when most participants are at their peak. By starting sessions at around 9 AM and going until 1 or 2 PM you catch the morning people and pick up the evening people halfway through a session. If you have a class from 1 PM to 5 PM, you can potentially pick up the evening people. Since it is unrealistic to be able to have only morning or evening people in your class, you have to improvise and build content and delivery for all learners. To do so, create materials and activities that stimulate and interest using such features as humor, movement, color, smells, regular review and other elements of brain-based and adult learning into your programs. For additional ideas, articles, and materials to accomplish this, visit www.presentationresources.net.

Preoccupation

Preoccupation can be caused by personal or other matters on a learner's mind (such as issues related to finance, school, marriage, family, or personal/work projects). When such factors are present, it is sometimes difficult for learners to focus on training content and expectations. This can frustrate you, the participant, and others in the classroom.

To help learners become more productive in the learning environment, try the following strategy.

 #146 Counsel the Learner

While it is not your role as a trainer to counsel attendees, you must do something if a learner's attention and lack of participation is creating challenges for you or problems for others in the class. To do this, you might take the participant aside and try to ascertain if their inattention is related to you, the program, or other participant's. If it falls into one of the categories defined in this chapter, then you might consider suggesting that the participant care of their issues and return to training when he or she can better focus, if this is possible. Suggest that a supervisor, organizational Employee Assistance Program (EAP) or counselor might be a resource if the issue relates to finances, mental well-being, health, substance abuse, marital and family problems, or workplace performance.

Faulty Assumptions

Faulty assumptions about training or educational classes are often based on past training experiences or encounters with other trainers or educators who have failed to meet the basic needs of learners. For example, many people who have not attended school for years or did not go beyond high school may rely only on their elementary and secondary school educational experiences (e.g., sitting in rows and having a teacher do all the work or talk "at" students). They may not realize that to be successful in a learning environment, they must become active participants and get involved in their own learning. Younger learners who have limited educational experience have little to compare to and may rely on perceptions passed on by others related to their role. To help all learners, try the following.

 #147 Encourage Involvement

Explain and demonstrate through your words and actions that learning will take place in an active format in your session. Plan activities throughout the program that engage and involve learners. Get them up, moving, and continually involved in the learning process. Build in games, interim reviews throughout the session, discussion and brainstorming opportunities, and other strategies for learners to become and stay engaged.

EXTERNAL OBSTACLES

Some barriers are out of your control, but you should still try to reduce or eliminate them when dealing with participants. Some typical examples might include the following.

Information Overload

Each day you and your learners are bombarded with information from many sources. You get information in meetings, over the radio and from television, from learners, and in a variety of public places.

In many instances, you and your learners spend as much as six to eight hours a day in a tightly scheduled learning environment with coworkers, peers, and strangers. Such overloads can result in added stress, inadequate time to deal with individual situations, distractions, and reduced levels of concentration. As a trainer or educator you can help increase learning effectiveness by focusing on what you do. The following strategy can help.

 #148 Streamline Material

With the time constraints in today's workplace and world most learners feel stretched to the point of breaking, your session content must be perceived as useful, efficiently presented, and value added. Anything less may turn learners off and impede potential learning. When designing program materials and content, look at everything with an eye to addressing learner needs. To determine the latter, do a needs assessment (e.g., focus groups, interviews, questionnaires, or other means) before designing the program to find out exactly what participants want and need to learn to enhance their knowledge and skills. Once in the session, continually monitor verbal and nonverbal reaction and participation throughout the program to ensure that you are providing what learners need. Do not forget to periodically do quick reviews (interim reviews) to ensure that content is working for learners and that they are getting key points. Also, do not fail to elicit feedback immediately after the session and later to determine if stated learning objectives were met and confirm that learners felt the time in training was well spent.

Other People Talking

For you to give your full attention to two sources or communicators simultaneously is not possible. To teach or train effectively, deal with only one participant at a time. Do not let multiple people try to talk at once. Enforce your classroom or training guidelines discussed earlier.

 #149 Control the Conversation

If someone else attempts to interrupt or speak while one participant or you are talking, smile, acknowledge them, and say, "Please hold your comment until _____ finishes." Or simply hold up your index finger to indicate "one minute" while you smile and continue to talk or listen to the other participant.

Office/Maintenance Equipment or Workers

Vacuum cleaners/ buffers, lawn mowers outside window, and other devices and contractors present in and around a training facility or classroom can be a distraction. Older projectors and equipment (e.g. television monitors) also emit quite a bit of humming or other noise.

To help reduce learning breakdowns and distractions, try the following strategy.

 #150 Plan to Eliminate Distractions

When possible, anticipate these irritants and ask the people responsible to limit or reschedule their use. If the noise starts once you are in session, take a short break while you find someone to speak with about the noise. If nothing else, try to find a more distant room from the noise and relocate your session during a break. If the offensive noise is from equipment you are using, try to find alternative resources. This is one of the reasons why you should rehearse your session in the actual room, using the actual equipment you will use during the session. This allows you to discover and remedy potential problems before trainees arrive.

Physical Barriers

Desks, counters, furniture, and other items separating you from your learners can cause psychological, as well as real, barriers between you and your learners. Depending on where you will be holding your training and the program content, this might cause a breakdown in effectiveness.

To reduce this possibility, try the following strategy.

 #151 Survey Learning Site in Advance

Like everything else in training, preparing in advance makes you appear more polished before learners. As a result, learning effectiveness is increased. It is important to identify and plan how to compensate for things such as supporting beams in the center of a room that interfere with vision and furniture that is not moveable, or is not the shape or size needed to allow small grouping or easy interaction. Ideally, you will be able to obtain an appropriately sized room for your group with the appropriate furnishings to meet planned activities and learning objectives. If this is not the case, you need to recognize such challenges before the session and plan to compensate for them. This may mean relocating to a different venue (if available), switching furniture, obtaining different audio visual aids, or simply rearranging furnishings to meet the needs of the session and group.

Failing to deal with physical barriers can sometimes nonverbally distance you from your audience or depersonalize your presentation. Be conscious of how you arrange your classroom so that you have access to learners and can move about the room comfortably and with ease. Ideally, no physical barriers will exist between you and your learners. This is one of the reasons why I typically use a smaller instructor's table in the front of the room or set up my table vertically toward the front of the room (see sample room layouts in Appendix C). I can then move closer to the learners without having a horizontal barrier to hide behind, as many instructors do.

CHAPTER 20

The Trainer's/
Teacher's Favorite

Some participants seem to go out of their way to get your attention and gain approval. This might be traced back to their wanting approval from parents as children or could be cultural as a show of respect for the teacher. Their efforts often manifest themselves in the form of continually raising a hand, volunteering assistance, or bringing gifts to you. I once had an older Hispanic student, in a Master of Arts class I taught, bring me an apple each week. She explained that in her culture and experience, this was a way of showing respect and appreciation for the knowledge I shared with her and others. Unfortunately, since such behavior is not common in Western cultures, her actions made me feel awkward and potentially gave incorrect perceptions to others in the class. Once I explained this to the student and told her that I appreciated her gesture, she stopped bringing the apple.

The challenge for you is to encourage the Trainer's Favorite to participate to acceptable levels without creating a distraction or alienating other learners. To do this, you have to analyze the behavior and try to figure out the participant's motivation for the behavior displayed. To effectively manage the behavior of the Trainer's/ Teacher's Favorite, try the following strategies:

#152 Thank the Learner

Initially, acknowledge the participant's efforts or contributions. Once you do so, turn your attention to others and gain their input or involvement.

 #153 Empower the Learner

Favorites often desire attention or have a need to feel that they are contributing to the learning experience. To satisfy this need, consider designating each as a small group leader, scribe (note taker), or spokesperson. The key is to make this selection seem random so that you do not appear to be condoning or contributing to their behavior (see Appendix E).

 #154 Avoid Eye Contact

In Western cultures, eye contact typically indicates interest, indicates that you are listening, and encourages participation from others. By avoiding eye contact with the Favorite, you do not encourage their input. Most importantly, you deny the learner opportunities to get attention, which is what that person often seeks.

 #155 Use Effective Body Positioning

Body language can be used to communicate powerful messages to your learners, including the fact that you are you are not attentive to their efforts. By standing with your back to the Favorite or facing in another direction, you can demonstrate your intention to ignore efforts to gain your attention.

Another position that sends a similar message is to stand on the opposite side pf the room, out of proximity with the Favorite. Couple these positions with Strategy #154 to make your point.

 #156 Address Their Behavior in Private

If the behavior being exhibited by the Favorite becomes distracting, you will need to deal with it proactively and positively. Take the learner aside during a break to discuss the situation. Thank the participant for contributions, but encourage him or her not to be so assertive. Encourage the participant to take a lower profile and allow others to volunteer or provide insights by appealing to a sense of "team" and stressing that when one person takes a very active role, others get lazy and often sit back to observe. Explain that it is a better learning environment when everyone provides input. Put all of this in terms of how much more the Favorite will also learn by letting others have involvement.

Latecomers

Effectively managing learning activities and staying on time is an important skill for trainers, facilitators, and educators. Unfortunately, many participants have not learned the importance and value of being punctual in arriving at a session or returning from a break. This problem can inhibit your ability to start, proceed, and end on time if you have not anticipated having such participants in a group. The following strategies can help maintain control of your planned activities even though some participants are not doing their part.

 #157 Set the Example

If you expect positive time management behavior from others, you need to act as a role model. Arrive at your sessions at least forty-five to sixty minutes early to greet learners and to ensure that everything needed is present, in order, and working. Also, return from breaks before to the announced time for restarting the session. Failure to adhere to these basic guidelines sends a message that it is okay for participants to come and go as they please with no sense of urgency.

#158 Start on Time

One of the best ways to demonstrate time expectations is for you to announce scheduled start times; then, punctually begin when those times arrive. By doing so, you communicate the importance of being on time and your expectations about maintaining an established schedule. Starting on time also demonstrates your respect for the time of your learners. It is unfair to have punctual participants wait for those less conscientious ones. Besides, if you wait for someone to show up and they fail to do so, you waste valuable training or teaching time.

 #159 Reward Punctual Behavior

Many experienced trainers, facilitators, and educators use a variety of rewards to recognize positive behavior of participants. You can announce the reward system that you will use at the beginning of the session. Select any method you desire to recognize punctual learners with some small item related to the session topic. For example, a toy with a smiling face for customer service training, a crossword puzzle for a decision-making or problem-solving class, or an inexpensive book related to the session topic. Note: You can often find the latter at major bookstore chains (e.g. Barnes & Noble, Book Star or Book Stop, or Borders in their clearance sections). The following are some of the techniques that I use. Many of these items can be used throughout a session to reward for other behaviors too (e.g., participation or volunteerism). You can find most of these items at www.presentationresources.net.

- *Playing Cards.* Randomly pass out one playing card to each participant who arrives on time, comes back from breaks punctually, or volunteers throughout the session. At the end of session, award a prize to the person with the highest hand of cards or score. Keep in mind that some religions prohibit gambling so cards might be offensive if you position them in a game of chance format.

■ *Carnival Tickets.* Similar to the card technique, pass out one numbered ticket/coupon to each punctual learner or volunteer. The rolls of coupons that have duplicates work best as you give one to the learner and keep one. At the end of the session, randomly draw one of the saved coupons and award a prize to the person holding the corresponding coupon.

■ *Stickers.* Place a colored dot, smiling face sticker, star, or other shaped sticker on participant name tents each time they arrive on time or otherwise demonstrate positive behaviors. The person with the most stickers at the end of the session wins a prize.

■ *Candy.* To provide an immediate reward for positive behavior, give returning participants a small piece of candy. Chocolate is often a favorite. (Hint: Brain-based learning researchers have found that peppermint stimulates the neurons in the brain).

■ *Other Countable Items.* Pass out whatever item you can think of that will result in a collection (quantity or total). For example, poker chips, play money, plastic coins, toothpicks, pennies, small erasers, or peanuts. With peanuts, let participants randomly select one from a bag, then at the end of the session, have them open the shells and count actual "nuts" from inside all their peanuts collected. Do not tell them in advance that you will be doing this, because they will look for larger nuts as they choose from the bag. This approach adds a bit of surprise at the end and can also break ties for most nuts. Award prizes for the person who has the most of an items at the end of the session. For prizes, I use a large burlap sack or pillowcase filled with a variety of toys, props, and incentives related to the session or class topic (e.g., stress balls, pins, or buttons with phrases tied to the session topic). When awarding things, I tell participants to reach into "Bob's Grab Bag of Goodies." Learners being awarded prizes get to reach in to select an item by feel. Another option is to display all award items on a table at the side or back of the room and let people either select an item or bid based on the number of counting items they have collected. Additionally, so that there are no "losers" I give everyone some small prize for participating (e.g., a "participant" ribbon, candy bar, or session related item).

 #160 Welcome Latecomers

Just because a person arrives late does not make that individual bad. There may be a valid reason for the tardiness (e.g., traffic accident, family emergency, or boss/client who calls them just before leaving for the class). As the latecomer enters, smile, briefly welcome him or her, direct them to a seat, provide any necessary materials, and assign them to a group (if appropriate). You or someone at their table can later help that person catch up with what was missed later.

The important thing is not to embarrass or ridicule the latecomer with sarcastic remarks (e.g., "Glad you could finally join us" or "NOW that _____ is here, we can get started"). This only causes resentment and creates a negative learning environment.

 #161 Assign Team Tasks

Before letting participants go on breaks or to lunch, assign them to teams (see Appendix D). Give them a task to complete upon returning from the break (e.g., discuss a course-related question, solve a riddle, or find a solution to a puzzle). Explain that the team that gets all members back on time and gets the right answer first will win a prize. This strategy applies the concept of peer pressure to help ensure everyone returns on time, because many people in the group are goal oriented and want to "win" so they will likely encourage their teammates to get back on time with the task completed. Others simply want to comply with the rules. This approach can also help in facilitating networking and communication between team members while adding a bit of fun, novelty and friendly competition.

CHAPTER 22

The Hyperactive Learner: Adult Attention-Deficit Disorder (ADD)/ Attention-Deficit Hyperactive Disorder (ADHD)

A DD/ADHD are complicated medical conditions that for years went undiagnosed, especially in adults. In many children, it is treated with stimulant drugs (e.g., Ritalin, Adderall, Dexedrine, and Cylert), behavior modification, and emotional counseling that are designed to help the person focus. In 1998, the U.S. government recognized ADD/ADHD as a legitimate medical condition covered under the Americans with Disabilities Act. Estimates by the National Institute of Health are that between 3 and 5 percent of children and 2 to 4 percent of adults have ADD/ADHD in the United States.

In the ADD/ADHD mind, thought organization favors multilevel activity in which the brain processes information simultaneously rather than in the linear fashion that most trainers use. ADD/ADHD is a genetic trait inherited from one or both parents. Some common behaviors for participants with ADD/ADHD are that they:

- Have trouble completing assignments in time because they lose focus;

- Have difficulty sustaining attention during activities;

- Make seemingly careless mistakes;

- Have difficulty organizing information during activities that require prioritizing or problem solving;

- Procrastinate on projects that require a lot of detail or complex thinking;

- Squirm in their seats, move frequently, or fidget (e.g., their crossed legs bounce continually and quickly);

- Have trouble recalling earlier information provided;

- Experience difficulty maintaining attention when spoken to directly or during presentations;

- Have trouble following through on instructions given.

The following are some strategies that can potentially assist learners with ADD/ADHD. Keep in mind that if someone tells you that he or she has this condition, the law requires accommodation in many situations. If you are aware of the condition and its symptoms, you can plan in advance to create material and activities that will address the needs of ADD/ADHD learners and others in the session without drawing undue attention or requiring additional effort in the classroom.

#162 Educate Yourself About ADD/ADHD

Many school systems provide information and training to teachers about ADD/ADHD, so that they are aware of the condition and how it manifests itself. As an adult trainer, you need to have such knowledge so that you can better meet the needs of all your learners. The Internet has lots of articles and information on the topic. Just type in Adult ADD or ADHD and begin learning about the condition.

 #163 Deliver Information in Multiple Formats

Because all of your participants gain information through one or more of three learning modalities (auditory, visual, or kinesthetic), and you may have some with ADD/ADHD, you should provide information in a variety of formats. You should plan some verbal delivery (e.g., lecture format, discussion, videotape, or audiotape), some visual delivery (visual aids and handouts) and some kinesthetic delivery (e.g., participant activities or hands on training aids). By providing handouts or posted guidelines on a flip chart, slide, or transparency with instructions for an activity while you explain verbally, you give learners a reference point to go back to if they have questions, missed a step, or just want to verify that they are on track for completion of the activity.

 #164 Provide Manipulatives on Tables

By placing small manipulative toys (e.g., foam balls, Koosh Balls®, flexible/bendable items, or Silly Putty®) (See Creative Presentation

Resources in the Resources for Trainers, Presenters and Educators section) on learner tables, you provide a kinesthetic outlet for energy. They can pick up and casually manipulate the items during the program. Such activity also sends you a nonverbal message that can indicate time for a break or change of pace in the program if you see many of your learners manipulating items.

 #165 Involve Learners

By changing the program pace with periodic activities every 8 to 10 minutes, you can help learners stay mentally alert. This can be done with question-and-answer periods, asking learners to provide examples of how they would apply material in their workplaces or lives, interim reviews of program content to that point to reinforce what was learned, or small group activities.

 #166 Adjust Your Presentation Style

Most people are products of their environments. This is especially true of learners with ADD/ADHD. If you are the type of high-energy person who continually speaks in a loud voice, paces back and forth, or gestures wildly throughout your session, you may cause similar reactions from your ADD/ADHD participants. You might even have undiagnosed ADD/ADHD yourself.

   To compensate and pace your presentation, videotape your session rehearsal to see what you are doing in front of a group. Make modifications that you might think appropriate so that you learn to speak in a more calming tone periodically. Move only with purpose to make a point, emphasize some element of the material or to position yourself at a different location during the program.

SECTION IV

Additional Issues

While many learner issues and types can be categorized, there are a few that stand alone. In this section, you will examine two additional types of learners that can create challenges in training and educational environments.

Substance Users

I n an era when drugs and alcohol are so readily available and pressures to perform at work are intense, it is not out of the realm of possibility that someone in your session is using some sort of drug or intoxicant. These may be legal or illegal drugs or could be alcohol consumed before or during a session. While the likelihood that this will be a major issue is slim, you should at least be prepared for the possibility.

 #167 Talk to the Learner

If you suspect that someone in your session is using drugs or alcohol quietly take them aside during a break. Some identifying factors indicating intoxication or drug use are an odor of alcohol, slurred speech, dilated (enlarged) pupils, erratic behavior, loud voice, verbal or physical combativeness. Any or all of these may be present depending on the severity of a participant's condition. It is important to recognize that some medical conditions can also result in some of these symptoms (e.g., diabetic crisis or diabetic ketoacidosis) do not jump to any conclusions.

#168 Call for Assistance

If you suspect that someone is indeed under the influence of some-thing, ask that person to leave the session and return to his or her office. If the person become boisterous or potentially violent, sum-mon assistance, security, or the police as appropriate. Depending on the person's condition and the location of the training or educational program (e.g., a hotel, resort, remote location off company property or school field trip), you might call for an escort or contact a super-visor, parent, or some responsible person (e.g. an adult in the instance of a younger learner or a spouse or adult in the instance of an adult) to pick the person up or call for appropriate transportation.

 #169 Document the Incident

Make sure that you note the time, date, name of the participant, orga-nizational information (e.g., department or company), a detailed description of behaviors, actions that you took, what was specifi-cally said by anyone involved, and the names and statements of witnesses, if appropriate.

 #170 Notify the Learner's Supervisor/
School Administrator/Parent

If the incident occurs at an organizational training function, notify the participant's supervisor of the situation and your actions so appropriate follow-up action can be taken. If on school or educational institution property, contact the Administrative office for guidance and assistance.

CHAPTER 24

Ill-Prepared Participants

If you have made preclass assignments only to have participants show up without them or with them not completed, you know the frustration of dealing with this issue. Precious classroom time then has to be spent with doing the work just for those few people who arrived unprepared. The following are some suggestions for dealing with this type of learner situation.

#171 Request Help From Supervisors/Parents

Unless you have direct control over learners in the workplace or school, you will need the help of someone who does to make sure that pre-class assignments are completed by participants. I typically deliver any assignment to supervisors with detailed instructions and ask them to administer and oversee them. If something needs to be completed and collected (e.g., a behavioral styles assessment), I ask that the supervisor collect them and return them to me before training. By getting the supervisor actively involved in the learning process you get them to buy in and gain post-training support. Your can also use them to emphasize the importance of the training to participants.

☺ #172 Stress the Importance of the Assignment

When sending correspondence or assiging pre-session tasks to learners, make sure that you stress the importance of completion in terms of what they will get (Added Value and Results for Me [AVARFM]). Tell them how to do the assignment, the goal of it, and how they will benefit from the assignment. By doing this, you potentially get their buy in.

☺ #173 Reward Participants

When making assignments, let learners know of any reward system that you use to recognize their achievements. For example, the first learner to show up in training with the assignment complete will get _____. Each additional learner showing up with a completed assignment will get _____. To add a sense of intrigue, tell them the value of the prize without actually announcing what it is. Otherwise someone might look at the reward and say, I do not want or need one of those. For example, if you have a gift certificate to a local restaurant, you might say it is a $20.00 value without telling what it is.

☺ #174 Use a Team Approach

Consider making assignments by teams. Let participants know who their teammates are and that the team with a complete and most correct assignment will receive an award at the beginning of the class. A variation of this concept is to assign each person on the team a portion of the project and reward them as a team. This encourages team members to check in with their peers to verify progress and compare their individual pieces. Thus, an element of peer pressure is used to get the project done before training.

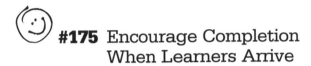

#175 Encourage Completion When Learners Arrive

Place reminders on flip charts or handouts positioned at learner locations before participants arrive. Encourage them to take out their assignment and review for completeness while they are waiting for others to arrive for the class. You might also encourage them to compare answers with peers, unless the assignments were a test of their knowledge or they each had different assignments or tasks.

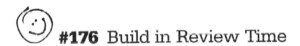

#176 Build in Review Time

Make the assumption that some people will not complete the assignment before class and build in a short period of time to review the assignment and answer questions at the beginning of the session.

SUMMARY

People are interesting and complex creatures who challenge any trainer, presenter, or educator. No matter what you know or think you know about human behavior, it is not enough to deal with every situation you will encounter in the classroom. Hopefully, as you gain more experience in dealing with different learning situations, you will also learn new skills and techniques to deal with virtually any type of trainee. This book provides just a beginning. It is up to you to become a "student of human nature" and learn as much as possible about how the human brain works, how outside factors such as education, experiences, values, beliefs, and other factors influence behavior, and some of the typical things that drive or motivate learners. If you do all of these things and apply what you have read, you should be on your way to providing an effective learning environment for yourself and all of your trainees.

Good Luck!

SECTION V
Appendices

This section provides additional tools, information, and resources that can assist in establishing a stimulating learning environment for various types of learners. These materials and ideas have been developed and used for a number of years and have proven valuable in my own training and educational sessions. The Web sites listed were active at the time of publication, however, like many things on the Internet, they change rapidly.

Sample Training Agreement

Please consider this program a "*safe*" environment—What we say here, stays here.

IT'S ALRIGHT TO . . .

- Express your ideas.
- Challenge the facilitator's ideas.
- Offer examples (please keep them generic with no names used).
- Question.
- Relax.

YOUR ROLE . . .

- Be on time (from breaks and lunch).
- Participate.
- Learn in your own way.
- Provide honest, open feedback on evaluations.
- Enjoy yourself!

FACILITATOR'S ROLE . . .

- Start and end on time.
- Professionally facilitate the exchange of information and knowledge.
- Allow time for and encourage your input.
- Listen non-defensively.
- Help you grow personally and professionally.

Abraham Maslow's Hierarchy of Needs Theory of Motivation

D r. Abraham Maslow studied workplace motivation of employees in the years following World War II. His research has been referenced and adapted many times over the years.

From a training or educational perspective, you can use the five levels of motivation that Maslow identified to focus your efforts in encouraging learners to accomplish established learning goals and to reward them for successes. It is important to remember that what motivates one person does not necessarily motivate another. In fact, some motivators might actually demotivate a learner (a theory offered by Frederick Herzberg).

The following are the five levels of need (from highest to lowest) in Maslow's Hierarchy of Needs, along with ways you can address each level for your learners. It is important to note that Maslow stressed that the basic needs must be fulfilled before any other level could be attained because they involve basic survival issues.

SELF-ACTUALIZATION

This is what the U.S. Army slogan of "Be all you can be" was all about. The premise was "Join us, we provide you with the tools and support to reach your maximum potential." To this end, as a trainer or educator, you must identify where learners hope to go as it relates to level of achievement in your sessions. Then, help them get there. This can be done through instruction, coaching, and providing tools and resources to allow them to succeed in implementing what they have learned in class, on the job, or in life.

ESTEEM/SELF-ESTEEM

This level of the hierarchy deals with personal ego, respect from others, self-respect, achievement, and recognition for efforts given. Most people want to be respected and appreciated by others. In a learning environment, you can address this need by deferring to someone's expertise or knowledge, recognizing accomplishments, and otherwise providing an environment where learners can feel the satisfaction of having others applaud accomplishments. You can also build in little accolades during learning in which participants cheer or applaud the efforts of someone who accomplishes something, offers a solution, or otherwise does something worthy or group recognition. A simple round of applause for a good response might be appropriate from time to time to meet this need.

SOCIAL/BELONGING

This level of Maslow's theory deals with love, acceptance, friendship, and companionship. As a trainer, facilitator, or educator you can address the need that many people have to socialize and feel part of a group by designing programs that have a number of opportunities for participants to interact with you and other learners. You can also include a networking period before or after training or class or have a group luncheon where learners can share ideas and commune. This might even be a "working lunch" in which participants are given assignments to find out things about others in the group to solve problems.

SAFETY OR SECURITY

This level of the hierarchy deals with physical as well as psychological safety and security. As a trainer or educator you can do common sense things like make sure that the environment contains no safety hazards, such as wires that are not taped down, broken furniture, boxes that can cause accidents, or equipment that might fall and injure someone. You can also provide mental security by explaining how the material covered will assist learners to become more effective and efficient in the workplace or other situations, thereby helping to solidify their position in the organization as a knowledgeable, skilled employee or individual.

BASIC/PHYSIOLOGICAL NEEDS

Maslow realized that people need to deal with the survival needs before they move on to any other levels of need. If they do not have the necessary food, clothing, water, shelter, and other crucial elements to survive, they are not likely to be concerned about learning new skills to qualify them for future jobs. Trainers and educators typically address basic needs by providing food and water throughout a session, adjusting temperature, allowing regular restroom or comfort breaks (at least every 60–90 minutes), and providing an adequate lunch period. They can also build training programs and class content that add value and that will help learners maintain their current jobs and ultimately move on to higher paying ones that will increase the amount of money they have available to satisfy basic needs.

Interactive Room Arrangements

The following images are from *The Creative Training Idea Book: Inspired Tips and Techniques for Effective and Engaging Learning,* also by Robert W. Lucas, published by AMACOM Books.

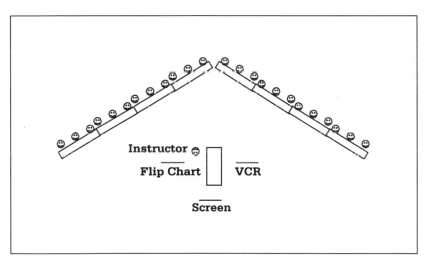

"V", Fishbone, or Chevron Style Seating (with tables using Overhead Projector)

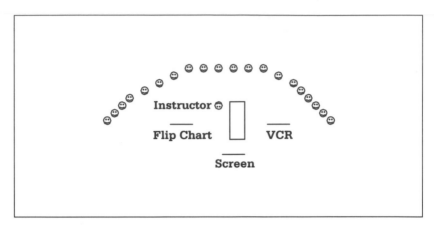

Crescent Style Seating (without tables using Overhead Projector)

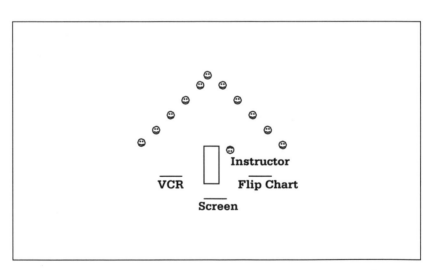

"V", Fishbone, or Chevron Style Seating (without tables using Overhead Projector)

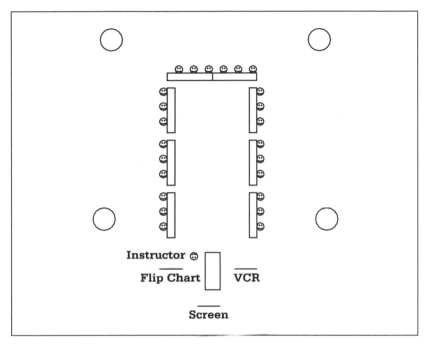

U-Shape Style Seating (with tables, breakout tables, and using Overhead Projector)

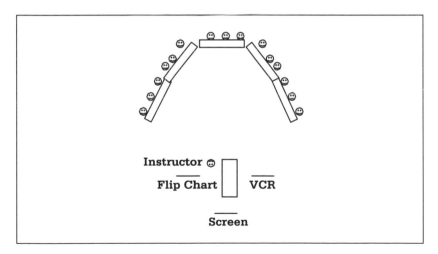

Crescent Style Seating (with tables—using Overhead Projector)

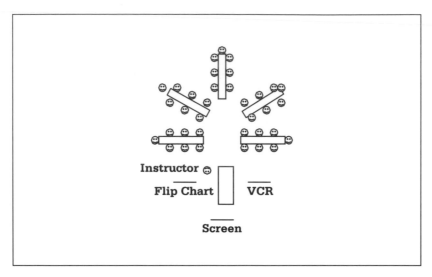

Horseshow Style Seating (with tables—using Overhead Projector)

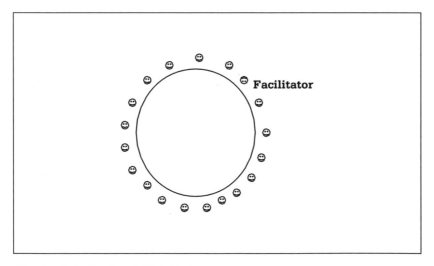

Circular Style Seating (with table)

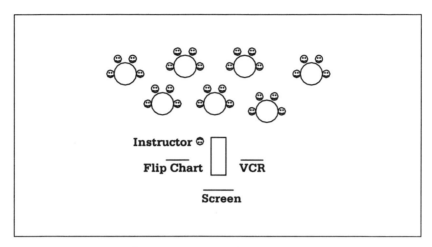

Satellite Rounds Style Seating (with tables)

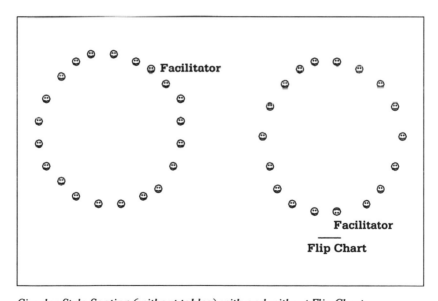

Circular Style Seating (without tables) with and without Flip Chart

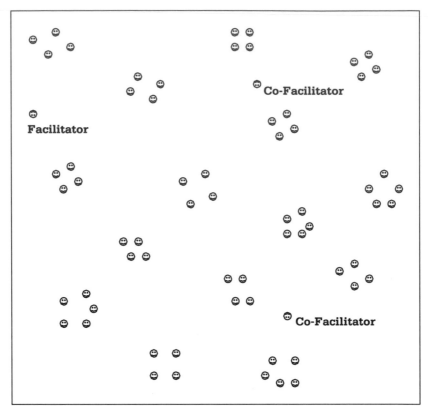

Cluster Style Seating (without tables)

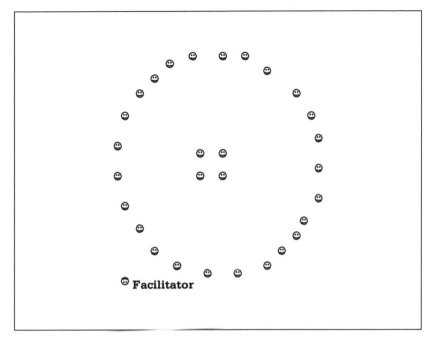

Fishbowl Style Seating (without tables)

Creative Strategies for Grouping Learners

PROPS/TOYS

Before learners arrive, decide how many activities you will use, how many groups you will need for each activity, and based on total participant number, how many people will be in each group. Once you have accomplished this, you are ready to think of ways to select participants for each group.

To introduce participants to the concept that you will be using props and techniques for grouping, emphasize at the beginning of a session that "we'll be using a variety of toys, games, and incentives to add a little FUN to the session." Tell them that they will find toys and other items on their tables that will be explained when the time comes to use them. Also tell them that the items are theirs to keep at the end of the session (if this is your intent). In doing this, you have functionality and reward rolled into one idea.

The following are some of the items that you can use in a variety of shapes and colors; often based on the course content (see Creative

Presentation Resources, Inc in Resources for Trainers, Educators, and Presenters).

■ *Props*

Props come in many forms ranging from actual items to toys, erasers, shapes, or other items. Here are some possible props for use in your learning environments.

—Actual or toy telephones are great for telephone and customer service training.

—Light bulbs enhance creativity and brainstorming sessions.

—Computers are perfect for software/PC training.

—Sail boats, cars, planes, or trains expand the theme in travel/transportation classes.

—Numbers and letters of the alphabet work for any topic area.

—Seasonal erasers can be used during a specific holiday or special day just to add a festive note (e.g., Halloween: ghosts, Thanksgiving: turkeys, Easter: bunnies).

—Dinosaurs work well when teaching change programs (reluctance to change).

—Jungle animals are great for stress and time management (especially if you can find ones in the shape of monkeys— to illustrate "keeping the monkey off your back").

—Ice cream cones relate to "licking the competition" or motivation.

—Crayon erasers can help focus attention of self improve- ment or goal setting (color your world).

—Star shapes tie nicely into motivation (you're a star).

■ *Small Toys*

—Smiling faced items can be used for customer service programs or virtually any other topic. For example, stuffed animals, hacky sacks, or foam balls.

—Currency or coins are effective for bank teller or cashier training or for rewarding effort.

—Fish exemplify successful programs/projects when things are "swimming along."

—Zoo animals can add fun to virtually any subject or when discussing stress or a high energy topic when things are hectic. (e.g., It's a zoo around here.)

—Insects or bugs help in activities when discussing pet peeves or things that "bug" participants either in customer interactions, or the workplace.

—Spinning tops made of plastic can emphasize high sales or improvement levels (on top of the world).

—Back scratchers made of wood or plastic can be related to ways of "reaching or attaining a goal."

—Sheriff's badges can be tied into concepts of taking charge, authority, or ownership of an issue.

—Ducks made of rubber or plastic might be used to remind people that sometimes things are not always what they are "quacked up" to be (when discussing problems or how things can go wrong in a specific situation).

—Hand held pencil sharpeners can point out the need to ask direct questions or "get to the point" when doing a customer service or interpersonal communication program.

—Footballs, baseballs, sponge balls, or similar small items may help emphasize teamwork or "getting on the ball."

RUBBER STAMPS

Stamps are very popular and come in hundreds of shapes. The nice thing about stamps is that they are fairly inexpensive and readily available. In fact, there are specialty stores entirely devoted to selling them. You can also purchase them at arts-and-craft stores, teacher supply stores, toy stores, and many department stores. In addition, you can custom design your own and have them made by many print shops. Just as with erasers and toys, you can use them to indicate group assignments. Simply stamp an image onto the participant's name tents before they arrive, and you are ready to go when the time for an activity comes around.

COLORED MARKERS

Other tools that can be used for grouping participants are colored flip chart markers. They provide a group identifier and, when ready to brainstorm, each person has a marker to write with on a flip chart. There are several ways to use markers when working in groups. The first technique is to indicate groupings by placing a series of colored markers at participant locations. For example, start with red for the first person, and then go around the room with blue, green, and black, then start over with the same color pattern until each person has a marker. You could then either group all like colors together for an activity or state that they have "X" number of minutes to form groups ensuring that all groups have a person with each color represented (e.g., one red, one blue, and so forth). Either way, you separate people who were sitting together and change the groupings.

A second use of for markers is to simply put a letter or number on name tents or nametags (e.g., A–F or number 1–6) depending on the size of groups desired. And a third approach is to use various colored markers and put a colored "dot" in the upper corner of each person's name tent or nametag. For example, the first person gets a red dot, the second a green, and so on until you have enough colors to meet your group size needs. You then repeat the pattern clockwise around the room until everyone has a colored dot.

Source: Lucas, R.W., *The Creative Training Idea Book: Inspired Tips and Techniques for Engaging and Effective Learning.* New York: AMACOM, 2003.

APPENDIX E

Creative Strategies for Selecting Volunteers

By randomly selecting people to assume various roles throughout your session, you reduce the likelihood that one or two people will dominate or control the session, discussions, and activities. You also encourage interaction and input by all participants.

To set the stage for participants playing an active role in the program, discuss the leader/scribe process at the beginning of your programs. It also helps when you plan to have small incentives (e.g., buttons, toys, candy, or other fun items) to give your "volunteers" and let them know this at the beginning. Doing so can actually generate some friendly competition as people rush to volunteer throughout the day.

In considering ways to involve people in activities, remember that some people are "private" and might become embarrassed if forced to take a lead role, or if they are put on the spot. It is also usually a good idea at the beginning of a session to identify trainer and participant expectations in some way. One of these means might be to state that if a participant does not want to take a leadership role or volunteer, they can "pass" without being embarrassed. When you are ready to select small group spokespersons (leaders) and note

187

takers (scribes), use your imagination to make the even fun and add a little interaction and activity to the session. Just as with grouping participants, this task is limited only by your imagination and desire to think outside the box.

The following are some possible ways to randomly select "volunteers" (see Creative Presentation Resources, Inc in Resources for Trainers, Educators and Presenters for additional props, articles, and ideas).

DIE OR COLOR CUBE

Die

One really random technique involves placing a regular or large foam rubber die on each group's table. Instruct the participants in each group to roll the die in turn, with the first person to get a "six" first becoming the leader. Have them continue until someone gets a "one." This person has then volunteered to be the scribe.

Color Cube

A variation on the die is to use a *color cube,* which has different colors (instead of numbers). Designate the color that will determine both the leader and scribe and have participants start rolling until someone gets them.

STICKERS

As with the technique for using various types of stickers to designate group members, you can also designate leaders and scribes in similar fashion. The easiest way is to use colored or themed stickers on name tents as described earlier. To appoint leaders and scribes, either use a larger version of the stickers or a second sticker added to various name tents for each group. You may even want to put the extra sticker underneath the folded name tent out of sight. Some "seasoned" session attendees may see the dual stickers and shy away figuring that they must be there for a reason.

MARKERS

By placing identifying marks (e.g., letters, numbers, dots, and symbols) on participant name tents or nametags, you can easily designate certain individuals from each group to play specific roles.

TOYS/ PROPS

As with the use of various items to identify team members, you can also designate leaders by placing special items at their seat location. These items might be the same thing everyone has, only differently colored, or they may be completely unique. By using a "symbol of office" you can even have a bit of fun by having the item passed from one volunteer to the next for various activities. The person with the "symbol" is visibly the leader or scribe. These items might be a special marker (e.g. Jumbo size) for the scribe, or a special toy for the leader (e.g.. magic wand, paper crown, or some other item associated with authority or power).

IDENTIFYING TRAITS OR CHARACTERISTICS

There are dozens of traits or characteristics about participants that can be used to designate them for specific tasks. However, be cautious not to choose something that will embarrass an individual, such as a physical characteristic that they cannot change (e.g., weight, height, nose/shoe size, or eye/hair color). Nor should you focus on items related to a group that they represent (e.g., religion, sexual preference, or race). This latter practice might even lead to charges of discrimination or favoritism.

Some more acceptable possibilities include:

- Birth date closest to or furthest from the date of your program
- Most/least pets
- Longest/shortest time with organization
- Person who most recently purchased as particular items (e.g., car, electrical appliance, piece of clothing)
- Person with the most of an item or color on their person
- Person with the most coins
- Person with the most/least siblings
- Person who traveled farthest/least to get to the program location
- Person with decorative metal on their shoes
- Person who has most recently participated in an athletic event
- Person who has had the most cups of coffee/tea/juice since arriving at the session
- Person with most/least letters in their first or last name
- Person with longest middle name
- Person born in the city in which the program is being conducted
- Person who has most recently attended another professional development program

Source: Lucas, R.W., *The Creative Training Idea Book: Inspired Tips and Techniques for Engaging and Effective Learning.* New York: AMACOM, 2003.

Recognizing Potentially Violent Learners

According to research by the National Institute for Occupational Safety and Health (NIOSH), "Violence is a substantial contributor to occupational injury and death, and homicide has become the second leading cause of occupational injury death. Each week, an average of 20 workers are murdered and 18,000 assaulted while at work or on duty. Nonfatal assaults result in millions of lost workdays and cost workers millions of dollars in lost wages." Obviously, these figures indicate an issue worth being aware of and being concerned about.

A number factors are contributing to this escalating trend. The culture of the workplace and worker values and needs have changed dramatically due to many factors (*e.g.* changes in organizational structure, diversity, technology, and increased job demands). Other external factors are also adding fuel to this smoldering fire (*e.g.* substance abuse, world issues, shifting societal values and beliefs, illegal drugs, violence on television and in movies, and a general trend to lash out at others in the form of verbal or physical assault, such as road rage).

Many law enforcement and private organizations have sought to identify a profile of potentially dangerous people in the workplace, based on previous offenders. The following are offered for your awareness, not to make you suspicious of learners who simply become emotional over an issue or topic. Also, keep in mind that due to many factors, such as issues going on in someone's life when you encounter him or her, anyone could potentially become violent under the right circumstances.

Some general characteristics of offenders are:

■ White male between 35–45 years of age.

■ A loner with few friends and little family contact.

■ Takes constructive feedback or criticism poorly.

■ Interested in firearms and other weapons.

■ Identifies or talks about violence.

■ Fails to take responsibility or blame when errors occur.

■ May use drugs and/or alcohol.

■ A history of work/job change.

Many people who are prone to violence exhibit telltale behaviors, that when viewed in totality, should be a warning sign for you and those around you. You are likely not going to encounter such a learner in your classroom. However, by being vigilant, you can possibly head off trouble by changing your approach to dealing with a possible offender, or at least reporting the behavior that you observe to a supervisor, team leader, human resources, and/or security.

Resources for Trainers, Educators, and Presenters

The items and vendors listed in this section are provided for your reference and possible use. Accuracy of information was current at the time of publication, but the author and publisher cannot be held responsible for changes that occur as organizations revise their business strategies and operational processes. The author and publisher do not endorse these organizations or their products and services. Creative Presentation Resources, Inc., is the exception, in that it is owned by the author, who stands behind its products and services.

PRODUCTS AND MATERIALS

CREATIVE PRESENTATION RESOURCES, INC.
P.O. Box 180487
Casselberry, Florida 32718-0487
(800)308-0399/(407)695-5535
Fax: (407)695-7447
www.presentationresources.net

Toys, games, incentives, videos, books, music, props, training and presentation aids, music, and props

MICROSOFT
www.microsoft.com/enable/productions
Free *Enable* video

BOOKS
Activities and Games

Arch, D. *Tricks for Trainers: 57 Tricks and Teasers Guaranteed to Add Magic to Your Presentations.* Minneapolis, MN.: Resources for Organizations, 1993.

Battaglia, P. *So You Think You're Smart: 150 Fun and Challenging Brain Teasers.* Blue Ridge Summit, PA.: Tab Books, 1988.

Brandreft, G. *The Great Book of Optical Illusions.* New York: Sterling Publishing, 1985.

Jensen, E. *Trainer's Bonanza: Over 1000 Fabulous Tips & Tools.* San Diego: The Brain Store, 1998.

Newstrom, J.W. and Scannell, E.E. *Games Trainers Play: Experiential Learning Exercises.* New York: McGraw-Hill, 1980.

Paraquin, C.H. *The World's Best Optical Illusions.* New York: Sterling Publishing, 1987.

Pike, B. and Solem, L. *50 Creative Training Openers and Energizers.* San Francisco: Jossey-Bass/Pfeiffer, 2000.

Scannell, E.E. and Newstrom, J. *More Games Trainers Play: Experiential Learning Exercises.* New York: McGraw-Hill, 1983.

Scannell, E.E. and Newstrom, J. *Still More Games Trainers Play: Experiential Learning Exercises.* New York: McGraw-Hill, 1991.

Scannell, E.E. and Newstrom, J. *Even More Games Trainers Play: Experiential Learning Exercises.* New York: McGraw-Hill, 1994.

Scannell, E.E. and Newstrom, J. *The Big Book of Presentation Games.* New York: McGraw-Hill, 1998.

Scannell, E.E. and Newstrom, J. *The Big Book of Teambuilding Games.* New York: McGraw-Hill, 1998.

Snow, H. *Indoor/Outdoor team-Building Games for Trainers: Powerful Activities from the world of Adventure-Based Team-Building and ROPES Courses.* New York: McGraw-Hill, 1997.

Solem, L. and Pike, B. *50 Creative Training Closers.* San Francisco: Jossey-Bass/Pfeiffer, 1997.

Sugar, S. and Takacs, G. *Games That Teach Teams.* San Francisco: Jossey-Bass/Pfeiffer, 2000.

Summers, G.J. *The Great Book of Mind Teasers & Mind Puzzles.* New York: Sterling Publishing, 1996.

Thiagarajan, S. and Parker, E. *Teamwork & Teamplay: Games and Activities for Building and Training Teams.* San Francisco: Jossey-Bass/Pfeiffer, 1999.

Ukens, L.L. *Energize Your Audience: 75 Quick Activities That Get Them Started and Keep Them Going.* San Francisco: Jossey-Bass/Pfeiffer, 2000.

Wujec, T. *Five Star Mind: Games & Puzzles to Stimulate Your Creativity & Imagination.* New York: Doubleday, 1995.

Adult Learning, Learning, and Intelligence

Bransford, J.D., Brown, A.L., and Cocking, R.R. *How People Learn: Brain, Mind, Experience and School.* Washington, D.C.: National Academy Press, 2000.

Caroselli, M. *Memory Tips for the Forgetful.* Irvine, CA.: Richard Chang Associates, 1999.

Dryden, G. and Vos, J. *The Learning Revolution: To Change the Way the World Learns.* Torrance, CA.: The Learning Web, 1999.

Gardner, H. *Multiple Intelligences: The Theory in Practice.* New York: Basic Books, 1993.

Hayes, E. and Flannery, D.D. *Women as Learners: The Significance of Gender in Adult Learning.* San Francisco: Jossey Bass, 2000.

Knowles, M. *The Adult Learner: A Neglected Species.* Houston, TX.: Gulf Publishing, 1984.

Knowles, M. S., Holten, E.F., III, and Swanson, R.A., *The Adult Learner.* 5th ed. Woburn, MA.: Butterworth-Heinemann, 1998.

Merriam, S.B. and Caffarella, R.S. *Learning in Adulthood: A Comprehensive Guide.* San Francisco: Jossey Bass, 1999.

Appearance and Image

Bixler, S. and Nix-Rice, N. *The New Professional Image: From Business to the Ultimate Power Look.* Avon, MA.: Adams Media, 1997.

Malloy, J.T. *New Woman's Dress for Success.* New York: Warner Books, 1996.

Maysonave, S. *Casual Power: How to Power Up Your Nonverbal Communication and Dress for Success.* Austin, TX.: Bright Books, 1999.

Weber, M. *Dress Casually for Success . . . for Men.* New York: McGraw-Hill, 1996.

Wetzel, K. and Harmeyer, K. *Mind Games: The Aging Mind and How to Keep It Healthy.* Albany, N.Y.: Thomson Learning, 2000.

Brain-based and Active Learning

Dennison, P.E. and Dennison, G.E. *Brain Gym.* Ventura, CA.: Edu-Kinesthetics, 1994.

Hall, D. *Jump Start Your Brain.* New York: Warner Books, 1995.

Hannaford, C. *Smart Moves: Why Learning is NOT All in Your Head.* Arlington, VA.: Great Ocean Publishers, 1995.

Hannaford, C. *The Dominance Factor: How Knowing Your Dominant Eye, Ear, Brain, Hand & Foot Can Improve Your Learning.* Arlington, VA.: Great Ocean Publishers, 1997.

Herrmann, N. *The Creative Brain.* Lake Lure, N.C.: The Ned Herrmann Group, 1995.

Ivy, D.K. and Backland, P. *Exploring Gender Speak: Personal Effectiveness in Gender Learning.* New York: McGraw-Hill, 1994.

Jensen, E. *Super Teaching.* San Diego: The Brain Store, 1995.

Jensen, E. *Brain-Based Learning.* Delmar, CA.: Turning Point, 1996.

Jensen, E. *Sizzle and Substance: Presenting with the Brain in Mind.* San Diego: The Brain Store, 1998.

Pierce, H.J. *The Owner's Manual for the Brain: Everyday Applications from Mind-Brain Research.* 2nd ed. Marietta, GA.: Bard Press, 2000.

Race, P. and Smith, B. *500 Tips for Trainers.* Houston, TX.: Gulf Publishing, 1996.

Rose, C. and Nicholl, M.J. *Accelerated Learning for the 21st Century: The Six-Step Plan to Unlock Your Master-Mind.* New York: Dell Publishing, 1997.

Silverman, M. *101 Ways to Make Training Active.* San Diego: Pfeiffer & Co., 1995.

Sylwester, R. *A Celebration of Neurons: An Educator's Guide to the Brain.* Alexandria, VA.: ASCD, 1995.

Environment

Wolverton, B.C. *How to Grow Fresh Air: 50 Houseplants That Purify Your Home and Office.* New York: Penguin Books, 1997.

Graphics and Design

Backer, L. and Deck, M. *The Presenter's EZ Graphics Kit: A Guide for the Artistically Challenged.* St. Louis, MO.: Mosby, 1996.

Bromley, K., Irwin-DeVitis, L., and Modlo, M. *Graphic Organizers: Visual Strategies for Active Learning.* New York: Scholastic Professional Books, 1995.

Frank, D. *Terrific Training Materials: High Impact Graphic Designs for Workbooks, Handouts, Instructor Guides and Job Aids.* Amherst, MA.: HRDPress, 1996.

Griffin, G. and Walker, K. *How to Draw Funny Faces.* Chicago: Kidsbooks, 1999.

Kearny, L. *Graphics for Presenters: Getting Your Ideas Across.* Menlo Park, CA.: Crisp Publications, 1996.

Lucas, R.W. *The Big Book of Flip Charts.* New York: McGraw-Hill, 1999.

Rabb, M.Y. *The Presentation Design Book: Projecting a Good Image With Your Desktop Computer.* Chapel Hill, N.C.: Ventura Press, 1990.

Raines, C. *Visual Aids in Business: A Guide for Effective Presentations.* Los Altos, CA.: Crisp Publications, 1989.

Robertson, B. *How to Draw Charts and Diagrams.* Cincinnati, OH.: North Light Books, 1988.

Rosen, M. and Kurzban, S. *Puzzle Makers Handbook: How to Create and Market Your Own Crosswords and Other Word Puzzles.* New York: Random House, 1995.

Sonneman, M.R. *Beyond Words: A Guide to Drawing Out Ideas.* Berkeley, CA.: Ten Speed Press, 1997.

Tollison, H. *Cartooning.* Tustin, CA.: Walter Foster, 1989.

Wescott, J. and Hammond Landau, J. *A Picture's Worth 1000 Words: A Workbook for Visual Communication.* San Francisco: Jossey-Bass/Pfeiffer, 1997.

Zelazny, G. *Say It With Charts: The Executive's Guide to Visual Communication.* 3rd ed. New York: McGraw-Hill, 1996.

Training and Communicating with Diverse Audiences

Axtell, R.A. *Gestures: The DO's and TABOOs of Body Language Around the World.* New York: John Wiley & Sons, 1991, 1995.

Dresser, N. *Multicultural Manners: New Rules of Etiquette for a Changing World.* New York: John Wiley & Sons, 1996.

Foster, J. *How to Get Ideas.* San Francisco: Berrett-Koehler, 1996.

Gray, J. *Men are from Mars, Women are from Venus: A Practical Guide for Improving Communication and Getting What Your Want in Relationships.* New York: Harper Collins, 1992.

Maloff, C., and Wood, S.M. *Business and Social Etiquette with Disabled People: A Guide to Getting Along with Person's Who Have Impairments of Mobility, Vision, Hearing, or Speech.* Springfield, MA.: Charles C. Thomas, 1988.

Morris, D. *Bodytalk: The Meaning of Human Gestures.* New York: Crown Trade Paperbacks, 1994.

Morrison, T., Conaway, W.A., and Boren, G.A. *Kiss, Bow, or Shake Hands.* Holbrook, MA.: Adams Media Corporation, 1994.

Reardon, K.K. *They Don't get It, Do They? Communication in the Workplace—Closing the Gap Between Women and Men.* Boston: Little, Brown and Company, 1995.

Tannen, D. *You Just Don't Understand: Women and Men in Conversation.* New York: Ballantine Books, 1990.

Tannen, D. *Talking from 9to5—Women and Men in the Workplace: Language, Sex and Power.* New York: Avon Books, 1994.

Tracey, W.R. *Training Employees With Disabilities: Strategies to Enhance Learning and Development for an Expanding Part of Your Workforce.* New York: AMACOM, 1995.

Van Gundy, A.B. *Brain Boosters for Business Advantage: Ticklers, Grab Bags, Blue Skies, and Other Bionic Ideas.* San Diego: Pfeiffer & Company, 1995.

Wolfgang, A. *Everybody's Guide to People Watching.* Yarmouth, MA.: Intercultural Press, 1995.

Creativity and Creative Problem-Solving

Ayan, J. *Aha!:10 Ways to Free Your Creative Spirit and Find Great Ideas.* New York: Three Rivers Press, 1997.

Buzan, T. *The Mind Map Book—Radiant Thinking.* London: BBC, 1993.

Forbes, R. *The Creative Problem Solvers Toolbox: A Complete Course in the Art of Getting Solutions to Problems of Any Kind.* Portland, OR.: Solutions Through Innovation, 1993.

Higgins, J.M. *101 Creative Problem Solving Techniques: The Handbook of New Ideas for Business.* Winter Park, FL.: The New Management Publishing Company, 1994.

Leonard, D. and Swap, W. *When Sparks Fly: Igniting Creativity with Groups.* Boston: Harvard Business School Press, 1999.

Mattimore, B.W. *99% Inspiration: Tips, Tales & Techniques for Liberating Your Business Creativity.* New York: AMACOM, 1994.

Michalko, M. *Thinkertoys: A Handbook of Business Creativity for the 90s.* Berkeley, CA.: Ten Speed Press, 1991.

Von Oech, R. *A Whack on the Side of the Head.* New York: Warner, 1990.

Motivation

Kohn, A. *Punished by Rewards: The Trouble with Gold Stars, Incentive Plans, As, Praise and Other Bribes.* Boston: Houghton Mifflin, 1993.

Music

Campbell, D. *The Mozart Effect.* New York: Avon Books, 1997.

Jensen, E. *Music with the Brain in Mind.* San Diego: The Brain Store, 2000.

Millbower, L. *Training With a Beat.* Sterling, VA.: Stylus Publishing, 2000.

Vos, J. *The Music Revolution.* Auckland, New Zealand: Learning Web, 1999.

Resources Related to Working with Difficult Participants/ Learners and People

The following is a list of Web sites listing courses, seminars and other resources for dealing with difficult behavior and situations. They were active sites as of 1/28/04. These sources are provided only as a reference and are not owned or endorsed by the author or publisher.

Dealing with Participants/Learners

www.wm.edu/TTAC/articles/challenging/interventions.html

www.work911.com/products/i-cdif.htm

www.nationalserviceresources.org/documentdb/index.php?action=detail&document_id=216?search_term=conflict%20resolution&m=all

www.janebluestein.com/wfed.html#Anchor-difficult

www.tregistry.com/NS_trtr.htm

www.universitytraining.com/mct.htm

www.nmsa.org/annualconf2003/pre_conference.html

www.users.qwest.net/~wwahec/manual/dealing.htm

www.cornwall.gov.uk/Consultation/focus5.htm

www.okea.org/TL/TLTrainings.htm

www.une.edu/cas/education/video.html

www.suntimes.co.za/2001/08/05/readright/edu07.htm

www.vanderbilt.edu/HRS/general/monthlyclasses.htm

http://web.grcc.cc.mi.us/btt/organization/orgd115.htm

www.edualliance.org/readytolearn/sessions/support.html

www.astroleague.org/al/socaids/leadship/leadrun.html

http://cit.hr.caltech.edu/Education/super&non_super/
presentations.htm

www.pitt.edu/~ciddeweb/FACULTY-DEVELOPMENT/FDS/
tawork_sp2002.htm#difficult

www.sitra.org/training/showcourse.php?courseid=254

http://sdps.ucdavis.edu/browse/ss/ss0020.htm

www.shu.ac.uk/services/facilities/dept/finmgt/training/
difficult.htm

www.northwestern.edu/hr/training/workplace.html#customer

www.state.mt.us/doa/spd/css/training/pdc/CatalogD.asp

www.thetrainingclinic.com/training2002/vnu%20schedule.htm

www.plsweb.com/sec03_graduate/courses/sylpride.htm

www.services.unimelb.edu.au/counsel/services/campus/
staff_workshops/situations.html

www.uswaves.org/index%5B1%5Dconfinfo.html

http://ulysses.carthage.edu/adulted/ccet.html#fall

www.peerlearning.ac.uk/assets/applets/
Dealing_with_difficult_incidents.pdf

www.peerlearning.ac.uk/html/training_leaders.html

www.extension.iastate.edu/communities/facilitate2.html

www.acu.ac.uk/adverts/academic_update/sept2001/
bookreview.html

http://csf.colorado.edu/forums/consbio/2002/msg00156.html

www-1.gsb.columbia.edu/execed/pdfs/migd.pdf

www.extension.ualberta.ca/cace/

www.nationalserviceresources.org/documentdb/
index.php?action=detail&document_id=216?search_term=
conflict%20resolution&m=all

DEALING WITH PEOPLE IN GENERAL

www.amazon.com/exec/obidos/ASIN/0028633709/
103-9726499-4557409

www.amazon.com/exec/obidos/ASIN/0968372244/
103-9726499-4557409

www.uri.edu/pdlot/t1su03.html

www.brandeis.edu/its/workshops/enroll_gen.php?
workshop_id=148

http://employ.uchc.edu/training/pdf/TRaining%20Manual.pdf

www.patrickdonadio.com/conducting_meetings.htm

www.uscg.mil/css/worklife/eap_training_programs.htm

www.enterprise-tc.com/docs1/docs_new/com6a.htm

www.shu.ac.uk/services/facilities/dept/finmgt/training/
difficult.htm

www.ombuds-toa.org/specialty_training.htm#Communicating
%20Across%20Cultures

www.acerra.ca/english/management/workshops/
dealingwithdifficultpeople.html

www.hughesconsultinggrp.com/TrainDev.html

www.vraweb.org/2003conference/programabstracts.html

www.unt.edu/cpe/roper/3.htm

www.plantops.umich.edu/building/Programs_and_Activities.html

http://search.yahoo.com/bin/search?p=dealing+with+difficult+
participants&ei=UTF-8

www.cilip.org.uk/training_events/cilip_courses/c30568.html

http://law.gsu.edu/CNCR/outreach/offerings.html

www.iabusnet.org/templates/main/search_action2a.cfm?
metakeyword=Human%20Resources

www.cornwall.gov.uk/Consultation/focus5.htm

www.utmem.edu/action/Training%20and%20Development
%20Registration%20Form%20_March_.pdf

www.insightinternational.com.au/itempage/33729.html

www.hr.duke.edu/train/communication.htm

www.pr.usm.edu/prnews/june03/nf620.htm

www.kcl.ac.uk/depsta/admsup/sdtu/Coursedetails/
perseffect.html

www.eriechamber.com/seminars_workshops.shtml

www.biz-assist.com/iframe.asp?topic=softskills

www.yorku.ca/hr/hrservices/trainingdevelopment/
comcsskills.html

http://attila.stevens-tech.edu/grab/gsa/LunchLearn.html#3

www.benwilliams.co.uk/tr_courses/tr_diffpeople.html

www.studentaffairs.com/onlinecourses/spring2003course3.html

ABOUT THE AUTHOR

B ob Lucas is President of Creative Presentation Resources, Inc, a training and presentation product company that distributes hundreds of toys, games, incentives, training aids, books, videos, and behavioral style surveys via its ecommerce site (www.presentation resources.net) to enhance learning environments and increase learning. In addition, Bob is also a founding Managing Partner in Global Performance Strategies LLC (www.globalperformancestrategies.com), a Human Resource Development training and consulting firm in the Orlando, Florida area.

Bob has gained extensive experience in human resources development, management and customer service over the past three decades in a variety of organizational environments by training and speaking to thousands of adult learners. This background gives him a real-world perspective on the application of theory he has studied, developed and used. He applies this knowledge as a consultant, trainer and adjunct university professor.

Bob focuses on assisting organizations and individuals develop innovative and practical strategies for improved workplace performance. Areas of expertise include presentation skills, training and management program development, train-the-trainer, interpersonal communication, adult learning, customer service, and employee and organizational development.

Currently, Bob serves on the board of the Central Florida Safety Council. He has served on the boards of the Metropolitan DC, Suncoast Chapter and Central Florida Chapter of American Society for Training and Development. He was the 1995 chapter President of the latter. He is also a regular presenter at the ASTD International Conference and has presented at the National International Alliance for Learning Conference.

Bob also serves as an adjunct faculty member for Webster University. In that position, he teaches Organizational and Interpersonal Communication, Diversity and Introduction to Training & Development and Introduction to Human Resource Development.

Listed in the *Professional Who's Who in the World, Who's Who in the World, Who's Who in America and Who's Who in the South & Southeast* for a number of years, Bob is an avid writer. He has authored eleven books and contributed to five professional compilations, including: *The Creative Training Idea Book: Inspired Tips and Techniques for Effective and Engaging Learning; The BIG Book of Flip Charts; How to be a Great Call Center Representative; Customer Service Skills & Concepts for Success; Job Strategies for New Employees; Communicating One-to-One: Making the Most of Interpersonal Relationships; Coaching Skills: A Guide for Supervisors; Effective Interpersonal Skills; Training Skills for Supervisors; Customer Service: Skills and Concepts for Business;* and *Customer Service: Building Successful Skills for the Twenty-First Century;* the *Annual: Developing Human Resources* series by Pfeiffer & Company since 1992 and to the HRDHandbook by HRD Press and the 2004 ASTD/Active Training compilation *Training and Performance Sourcebook.*

Bob has earned a Bachelor of Science degree in Law Enforcement from the University of Maryland, and a Master of Arts degree with a focus in Human Resources Development from George Mason University in Fairfax, Virginia.

Index

Past experiences, and present learning, 18
Patience, with older learners, 67
Peer pressure
    to handle experts, 110
    to handle latecomers, 150–151
    to handle show-offs, 105–106
People with disabilities, 5–7, 53–60
    assistance, unsolicited, 56
    equal treatment for, 55–56
    forms of address for, 6–7, 54
    hearing impairments, 56–57
    learning disabilities, 16
    mobility impairments, 59–60
    patronizing, avoiding, 55
    in population, 15–16, 53–54
    respect, actions of, 56
    trainer information on, 55
    visual impairments, 57–59
Personal issues, and distracted learners, 132–133, 135–136
Pessimists, 119–120
Physical activity, benefits of, 134
Physical barriers, and distracted learners, 140–141
Physiological needs, 171
Planning, 19–25
    of content/delivery, 22–25
    practicing training/delivery, 25
    rules for training sessions, 24
    of training environment, 21–22
Positive attitude, and communication, 8
Preparation of learners, ill-prepared learners, 161–164
Presentation methods, importance of, 21
Procrastination, and ADD/ADHD, 154
Props, uses of, 182–183, 189
Proximity to learner, to control learner behavior, 127–128
Psychological issues
    of distracted learners, 133–134
    mental fatigue, 17

Q
Questions
    of Baby Boomer generation, 74
    closed-ended questions, 31, 94–95
    eliciting from learners, 87
    of older learners, 67
    open-ended questions, 30–31, 46–47, 57
    to refocus learners, 90–91, 94–95

R
Relationship-building, words/phrases for, 8–9
Review
    benefits of, 88
    build in time for, 163
    interim reviews, 138
Revolutionaries, 117–118
Rewards
    to discourage autocratic learners, 124–125
    for punctuality, 148–150
    types of, 148–150
    for well-prepared learners, 162
Risk taking, and Y Generation learners, 79
Room arrangements, 173–179
Rubber stamps, uses of, 184
Rude behavior, inconsiderate learners, 99–103
Rules for training sessions
    for cell phone use, 88, 101
    examples of, 88
    for inappropriate talking, 87–88
    presenting, 24
    Training Agreement, 24, 122–123, 167

S
Safety needs, 171
Sarcasm, avoiding, 50
Seating, room arrangements, 173–179
Security needs, 171
Self-actualization, 170
Self-esteem, 170
Show-offs, handling of, 105–108
Shy learners, 97–98
Sign language, translators, 57
Silence
    as cultural value, 37–38, 44
    of World War II generation learners, 72
Social needs, 170–171
Speaking slowly
    for culturally different learners, 30, 45
    to improve listening, 85–86
Standard English, 37, 48
Stretching, benefits of, 134
Subject matter knowledge, 21
Substance users, actions to take, 159–160

T
Talking in class. *See* Inappropriate talking